Auditing Leadership

Auditing Leadership

The Professional and Leadership Skills You Need

BRIAN D. KUSH

WILEY

John Wiley & Sons, Inc.

Published by John Wiley & Sons, Inc., Hoboken, New Jersey.
Published simultaneously in Canada.

For general information on our other products and services, or technical support, please
contact our Customer Care Department within the United States at 800-762-2974, outside
the United States at 317-572-3993 or fax 317-572-4002.

Wiley also publishes its books in a variety of electronic formats. Some content that
appears in print may not be available in electronic books.

For more information about Wiley products, visit our Web site at www.wiley.com.

Library of Congress Cataloging-in-Publication Data:

Kush, Brian D.
  Auditing leadership : the professional and leadership skills you need / Brian D. Kush.
      p. cm.
  Includes index.
  ISBN 978-0-470-45001-7 (cloth)
  1. Leadership. 2. Auditors.   I. Title.
  HD57.7.K868 2009
  658.4′092–dc22

                                                                                    2009004124

Printed in the United States of America

10 9 8 7 6 5 4 3 2 1

Contents

Preface

This book was made to help YOU...ACHIEVE.

It was not written to give you all the answers. It certainly was not made to provide any technical auditing knowledge or know-how. It was not created to be an all-encompassing book on leadership skills for auditors. This book was also not made to define leadership. In fact, many of the skills and tips mentioned might not be considered "leadership" skills at all. It was also not made to provide you a list of the characteristics that make up a leader. There will also be little, if any, references to any auditing standards, FASBS, GASBS, EITFs, or any other technical references.

This book was created, however, to get you thinking about what leadership means to YOU, and what professional skills you want to develop and improve.

It was written to provide you with ideas, insights, and tips on the leadership and professional skills you will need to take your life and career to the next level. YOU choose the ones you can implement tomorrow. Some of these ideas and insights you have already heard, some you have not. Some you may disagree with or they may make you feel uncomfortable. That is good.

Our objective is to allow you to take some of the ideas referred to herein and the ideas you come to create by reading this book and reflecting on your current practices, and IMPLEMENT THEM AND, BY DOING SO, BECOME A BETTER LEADER, *a more reflective, aware, and intentional leader* of yourself and those you choose to lead, no matter your job or position.

Turn to page 225 right now. This is your implementation plan. Think about the end benefit of reading this book, from the very beginning. As you read it, think about how you will be filling out this last page.

Why was this book titled *Auditing Leadership*? Is this a book about leadership skills for auditors or is it a book about auditing your own leadership skills? Hopefully you agree that it is about both!

Some notes to help you in reading this book....

The chapters stand on their own:

> While some chapters may be related to others, and in some cases refer to other subjects mentioned in other areas of the book, this book was written so you could pick it up and read any chapter at any time. So read it cover to cover, or pick your reading based on a chapter that intrigues you that day.

Generic wording:

> We use certain words throughout the book, words like *partner* or *executive, manager, staff,* and *client.* We know some of you may be working for private companies, public companies, public accounting firms, or government entities. Most of the words are pretty universally accepted in the auditing world, but we know some organizations set up their titles differently, so keep in mind we use these words generically.
>
> The word *client* should be construed as the group, entity, or person under audit. If you work for a professional services firm, then it is your outside paying client. Some internal audit groups refer to those they audit as clients and that is how we will refer to them in this book.
>
> The words *partner* and *executive* are meant to describe the highest level at your organization and are interchangeable.

Some sections in certain chapters may be more geared toward external auditors and others may be more geared to internal auditors. You will probably notice that as you read. We still feel like you can benefit from these sections, and as I have come to realize, we may have some slight differences but auditors are still auditors. We are all the same species!

Born to Be Skeptical Sections

Auditors are a skeptical species. We are supposed to be that way. We are bred to be that way. It's a characteristic that serves us well in performing our jobs, and the auditing standards formally preach "professional skepticism" to us. As you read this book you will notice, from chapter to chapter, a few "Born to Be Skeptical" sections. What are these? When we present some ideas, we also know there may be another side, a questioning side to them. So what we have done is question some of the ideas presented in the sections, the very same ideas we have presented, and provided some answers or rebuttals to that skepticism.

About the Author

Brian D. Kush, CPA, CISA, is the President of Moxie Partners. He is the leadership and personal productivity coach hired by accountants and other knowledge workers in many of the country's leading accounting firms and other professional service organizations to help their people take their life and leadership skills to the next level.

Brian's clients uncover and live their values, purpose, and true potential as leaders through his positive, supportive, and curiosity-based coaching style. They save hours in their workweek and develop improved relationship and communications skills that lead to better-served colleagues and clients and more effective and profitable engagements.

Prior to being a leadership coach, Brian worked in the auditing industry and has been a consultant and trainer to both IT and financial auditors, having spent five years with Ernst & Young and eight years with Audit-Watch, Inc. He has worked intimately and consulted with employees at all levels, from level one all the way up to the executive/managing partner level, at hundreds of accounting firms and internal audit departments across the country.

Brian lives in Reston, Virginia, with his wife and son. He is the founder and author of the Healthy Accountant blog.

Auditing Leadership

PART I

Professional Interaction and Reflection Skills

CHAPTER 1

Where Are You Going?

How much time have you spent planning your life? How much time have you spent thinking about where you are headed? Do you know where you want to be in five years? Have you ever dreamed about how much you can achieve in the next 10 years? It does not matter if you are 20 or 60 years old, the questions are yours, and only yours, to answer. If you were to envision the most ideal scenario of where you would be and when, what does it look like? Many accountants I have met and worked with have not invested much time in planning their life and how to live out the most successful version of themselves they can visualize. Most people have not defined what that successful version looks like. They feel they are either too young (Why should I be thinking about that stuff now?), too busy (I have no time to plan my life, because I cannot even plan my day!), or too "stuck" (I do not have much control over what is going on in my life. I just do what is asked of me!).

It is very easy to ignore these things or not think about them. It is extremely easy to get stuck in the day-to-day responsibilities we maintain, and you cannot plan your life in one day or even a few days. Let's turn on your self-reflective mode for a little while and have you ask and answer some questions that will provide you with a base for planning the life you want and becoming the person you want to become. We are not talking solely about your career. We are talking about all aspects of your life and your future.

It is absolutely amazing how much you can achieve as an auditor when you are more self-aware and intentional about your growth. That is one of the reasons this book was written ... to uncork your potential.

This book is about being intentional, reflective, and proactive about the development of your leadership skills. It is about having a big plan and having lots of little plans. It is about never forgetting your big plan and always being able to forget your little plans. The skills discussed in this book are centered on your career in auditing, but they can be leveraged in many aspects of your life. Becoming a better leader does not pertain only to circumstances where you are leading a team; it pertains to all that you do, whether you are "leading" your family, working alone, or working with a large group of people.

Let's dive into you and take a grander view of what you stand for and desire to achieve. While achievements and new skill development are great and should be celebrated, the real value in specific achievements is how they help you to become the very authentic, successful person you desire to be, or maybe the person you already ARE but just have not realized yet. So now we want you to ask yourself this question: **Who is the person I desire to be, the person I already am (buried deep below the surface)?**

To answer this question, you should ask yourself a few questions about what matters most to you:

- What are the most important roles in your life you aspire to master?
- What is your mission?
- What are your core values?

Your Roles

Take some time to focus on and identify what you consider to be the most important roles in your life. Most people will limit the number of roles they uncover to five or less, not because there aren't more roles than that, but because limiting the number of possible roles will force you to think about the general and most important ones that you feel you have and want to excel in serving. The roles you identify will probably be centered on the most important responsibilities and relationships you have. Some examples are:

- Spouse
- Parent
- Friend
- Leader at work
- Community member

Now spend some quality time thinking about what each of these roles mean to you. Why are they important? How do you become wildly successful in fulfilling that role over time? How might others see you in this role? Spend some time pondering the role you have identified. Why is it important to you? How do you feel in serving that role to the best of your ability? Some people can complete this exercise rather quickly, while others will spend hours and maybe days thinking about it and documenting their thoughts. Let yourself go a little bit when answering these questions and uncovering your roles. Don't get caught up in judging your thoughts and feelings too quickly. There are no right and wrong answers here. Consider getting away to a place where you can do some real reflection. You are documenting the most important roles you live in your life. These roles ARE your life, and you will be spending a lot of your time in fulfilling them.

Here are examples from two of your fellow auditors. Keep in mind that neither of these was crafted in one sitting or in one day. It took time and many revisions to explore and refine these personal role definitions. Both of these people not only spent a few hours or more brainstorming what the role meant to them, they also went so far as to ask their family and friends for feedback and input. The input from others was very useful. It allowed them to see themselves through others' eyes. They both reported that the process of uncovering their roles and obtaining feedback from others was just as valuable as the documented end product. One of the auditors chooses to review this role on a weekly basis; the other on a daily basis. As they deemed necessary, both made changes to these role definitions since they first documented them.

Example 1: Family Guardian

"Currently, I am a single mother with two children. That brings challenges at times, some very difficult challenges. I see that as a blessing in my life, as it has taught me to be disciplined and hopeful at the same time. My children are very important to me and I serve my role in ways that provide for them financially, emotionally, and developmentally. The most important thing I do is spend time with them, both in terms of quantity and quality. Anyone can give them money, anyone can give them shelter, but nobody else can spend time with them as their mother like I can.

This role provides me inspiration to use all the time I have in the most efficient manner and to value quality time with my kids."

Example 2: Body Protector

"I choose to protect my body both physically and mentally, because I know it allows me to accomplish what I want to in life. It affects my relationship with my wife, and I cannot help but think of our future together and that being in good physical shape will allow me to enjoy a long and fulfilling life with her. By exercising regularly, I am energized on a daily basis. I take this role seriously."

Choosing your roles is a personal exercise and decision. Only you can do it. The more authentic it is to you, the better. One auditor chose, for example, to document her role as "Self-Server." That sounds kind of selfish, right? This person actually struggled with being selfish enough. She caught herself saying yes to everyone but herself, so she created an important role focused on being more aggressive about looking out for her interests. The surprising result (to her) was that by looking out more for herself, she actually became more energized to focus on her other roles, roles that affected others around her!

Another auditor chose "Volunteer" as one of her most important roles. She did serious reflection, received valuable feedback from friends, and realized this was a role she cared about and was already living. This role covered a lot of the work she did with charitable organizations. It also covered some things she did at work, including serving on a committee that leads the company's initiative to encourage employees to be involved in volunteer and charitable organizations.

Carefully choose your roles. If you are someone who spends a lot of time in your career, working hard at your job, one of your top roles will probably be related to that, or better yet, one or more of your roles is served every single day you show up to work.

Your Mission

Forget that you are an auditor for a second. Think about your personal mission in life. What is it? What is the BIG AUTHENTIC AGENDA that you have and want the world to witness? This may not be an easy question to answer. Your mission will not be easy to define right away. It may take some time ... time well spent. There are a number of ways you can go about identifying your personal mission. Here are a few:

    YOU ARE DEAD. It is the day of your funeral. People are sad. You are happy because you get to see everyone and listen into what they are saying. All the people you care about are there and they are talking about you in a joyous way. What is the most common thing people say about you and what is their tone? What do you want people to say about you? How do you want to be remembered so that EVERY single person there mentions the same qualities and ideals? They are all saying you lived for something and you really stood for something. It was a cause, but what was it?

    THINK ABOUT OTHER PEOPLES' MISSIONS. They may have one, they may not. Consider your doctor, for instance, or the doctor that cares for your spouse, or daughter, or brother. Doctors take care of the most important people in your life. Think about the doctor as a single person. What would you like this doctor's mission to be? You probably would not want it to be: **Become rich and buy the biggest house in the area by getting patients quickly in and out of my office and charging them the most money.** It would be something much more profound, deep, and meaningful. The mission statement would make you feel good about having your loved one's care under this doctor's direction. Some examples of what that doctor's mission statement could be include:

- To treat every human being who walks through my door as if they were my family
- To improve the health of every person I serve
- To help others realize their fullest healthy potential

Notice that those statements vary to a large degree, and though they are general, they could be used to help with day-to-day decisions and year-to-year goals. They provide overriding guidance on why this person wants to be a doctor and how he or she wants to feel at the end of each day in trying to serve the mission.

The doctor is a powerful emotional example of someone with whom you want to be associated in a meaningful way. Wouldn't you feel better about taking your family member to a doctor who has a mission statement like one of those listed?

Now start thinking about your own.

What is the one sentence you can create that will describe your mission? It is typically not a statement with a destination. It is not something you achieve one day and then you are done. It is something you can look at and ask yourself if you are achieving it EVERY DAY, living it EVERY DAY. It is a sentence that must have real meaning to you. The more authentic it is, the more powerful it will be to you. You must create it and then OWN it. This may take some time. In fact, you may be tweaking it for years. That is fine. Just spending some time in thinking about these things will get you started down a path in your life where YOU control how success is measured and where YOU can hold yourself accountable for living to YOUR standards.

The mission statements presented over the next two pages are examples provided so you can get a better feel for what is being illustrated here. They may help you create your mission statement, but one of these cannot be your mission statement, simply because it is not yours. Your statement must be written by you to be effective. It has to come from inside, and it has to be something that means so much to you that you are willing to fight for it. Don't worry if you cannot create one right away. It is very difficult to create a one-liner that is your mission statement. It takes a lot of time and thought.

Sometimes it's best to just start writing about what you care about most in life. Then you can extract your mission statement from those writings. This process works well for most people. First, write about yourself and what is important in your life. Maybe include a story of something that happened in your past, an event when you really felt high on life. Why was that? What can you extract from that story that helps you to realize what you stand for and what your "cause" is?

One auditor spent some time reflecting on her life and discovered a very powerful trait. She really enjoys teaching others. This was apparent to her during college, when she would help her friends study and provide tutoring to elementary school kids near her college. It also became apparent in her 10 years in the auditing profession, as she realized her favorite moments were helping younger auditors learn on the job. She frequently signed up to help her organization with internal learning initiatives, and recently she had begun teaching classes to interns and first-year staff at her company. She never spent the time to reflect on her attraction to teaching and helping others learn until she focused on her mission statement. So she came up with: **To help others learn and grow.**

Pretty simple, huh? What she REALLY likes about this mission is that she can expand it to so many parts of her life, and she realized she was already living her mission!

You may choose to be more specific in your mission statement by including more details about what matters to you. Here is a more detailed example, or a more general example, depending on how you look at it:

My purpose is to live life to the fullest by always listening to others, valuing all my experiences, and continuing to challenge myself to enhance the most important relationships in my life. When I look back on my life, I see someone who appreciated everything that was given to me. I made the most of the strengths I was given.

Note that a personal mission statement does not need to have "measurables" attached to it. Goals should be measurable, and goals might be helpful in aiding you to meticulously live your mission over short or long periods of time. A personal mission statement, however, is powerful because you can use it to challenge yourself EVERY DAY on how you are living it.

Some additional personal mission statement examples:

- To bring quality to everything I touch in helping to vanquish illiteracy from this world.
- To help small business owners succeed.
- To delight in helping others realize their full potential.
- Because I can.

The last one, "Because I can," might not make much sense to most of us. This person uncovered a great sense of purpose in helping others, but he liked the simple slogan "Because I can," which referred to how grateful he was for what he had in life and in turn he felt a great sense to help others simply "because he can." It was very authentic to him.

Your mission is about defining your purpose. The task of defining it, much less living it, is difficult enough but can be very rewarding and a personal guidance tool to challenge yourself to be the person you want to be. Start today!

Your Core Values

What are the characteristics that you value more than anything else? What characteristics are so important to you that you will sacrifice in order to live them?

So many things that are important to us can come and go. Achievements, awards, people, relationships, jobs, careers, and EVEN ROLES, the very same important roles that we discussed at the beginning of this chapter ... all those things can come and go. But the values that you hold true to yourself, that you honor and practice, that you stand for ... those can be present through your thoughts and your actions every single day, for the rest of your life.

Integrity is one of the most common values found on organizations' Web sites when they are describing their core values. But what does integrity mean? It sounds like a good thing, but until you can describe in detail what it means, it's nothing. So if the term "integrity" has been presented by a company as a value, ask yourself: Does every employee agree with that and does everyone in the organization truly value that characteristic, enough so that they are willing to sacrifice for it? It is actually easier to uncover personal values then those of an organization, because your personal values are YOURS alone.

Until you can describe a value in detail, you cannot hope to live it, or be formal about continuing to live it as one of your core values. It really does not matter what the specific dictionary definition is, just as it does not matter how other people might define a word that you use to describe one of your core values. All that matters is what it means to you. Below are some common examples:

- Honesty
- Creativity
- Audacity

- Loyalty
- Professionalism
- Appreciation
- Relationships
- Listening
- Courage
- Promptness
- Responsiveness
- Simplicity
- Enthusiasm

Many of those values sound honorable. You may WANT to have all of these as your core values, but that is not practical. A core value must be uncovered more than "adopted." You probably already have core values—a few characteristics that already mean something to you, something really important.

Consider asking those people close to you about their perception of your values. What are the few words they would use to describe you? Why? When and how did you exemplify the values they have listed for you? This exercise may be enlightening and empowering to you.

The list above is very short in comparison to the huge amount of values that are possible. What you need to do is understand and, if you choose, document what your values are, WHY YOUR values mean the most to you, and what types of things you do to practice these qualities. Below is a simple example of how to document and describe a core value:

Honesty: I put honesty above everything else. When I say something, it is always the truth.

Roles, Mission, Values: Tying It All Together

So why did we have you think about these three subjects? Even if you were able to put some serious thought into your roles, mission, and values, what does that have to do with your leadership skills and your life planning? EVERYTHING. When you are making your goals for any given year, when you are making big decisions in your life, it will be very useful to you to have these things defined and documented. It will help you bring purpose to everything you do. Revisit your role, mission, and values often. You may start to do it automatically when making decisions. Read through your core values when making BIG LIFE DECISIONS. We will also revisit them with you later in this book.

Leadership Summary

Your foundation for being a leader comes from uncovering who you are and what you stand for in your life, both inside and outside the office walls. Only you can do that. Uncovering what you see as the most important roles you serve, your core values, and your mission will provide a foundation to guide your actions and make decisions both big and small. These three things, when all is said and done with your life, will be your LEGACY.

CHAPTER 2

Selling Number One

Continuously Selling Yourself

Every time you do something in front of someone else or a group, you are putting yourself, your skills, your attitude, your professionalism up for sale. Basically you are selling yourself ("numero uno"), and the better you do it, the more other people are interested in you . . . your ideas, your persuasions, and your opinions.

You are selling when working with clients, with colleagues, with your family, with your friends . . . **all the time.**

Have you ever been in a meeting and noticed that there are one or two people to whom nobody listens? Is it always because they are incompetent? You may say it's because they are quiet or simply introverted. Sure, that could be true, but many quiet, introverted people can still command attention when they do speak up to others. So maybe it is something more. Many times, that something is that the speaker has not done a good job of selling themselves. Nobody is "sold," so nobody listens.

We sell ourselves during all different types of communications. As auditors, we have to sell ideas a lot more than we probably realize. Some examples:

- Selling the idea of the client completing a schedule in the right way
- Selling the idea that a transaction needs to be accounted for differently
- Selling the idea that a staff member should stay late and complete her open items

Beyond just selling ideas during live conversations, we sell ourselves using other mediums as well.

We Sell Ourselves in E-mails We Create

- Be brief and professional.

- End the e-mail professionally. Have you ever debated someone about the importance or unimportance of signing every e-mail with your name at the end? Do you have to in each case?
- Is there a difference between signing Ted Auditor, Ted, or simply "—T"? Maybe, maybe not.

Consider the person receiving the e-mail. You are selling to a particular person, so consider that particular person when sweating the small stuff like your signature. A "—T" might be expected for a friend, but not for a new client. I have heard a lot of accountants say they would prefer to err on the side of being too formal; that seems like a reasonable approach.

Remember, you are selling yourself with the e-mails you send. The clarity of your e-mails adds to your professional image. Before sending, reread your longer e-mails to see if they can be shortened or clarified. Get to the point. Also, do not forget that it is certainly acceptable to use bullet points and numbered lists in e-mails.

We Sell Ourselves in the Voicemails We Leave

Once again, be brief and professional. I have heard some people say they script important voicemails. If you are not great at leaving short, professional voicemails, try scripting one ahead of time. If it is really important, take a practice run. You will get better.

We Even Sell Ourselves in the Voicemail Greetings We Record

Auditors are judges. That is what we do. This could not be more apparent in the constant judging of our voicemail greetings. And the chances are the people who will be hearing your greeting the most frequently are fellow auditors!

Have you ever received a comment on your greeting? I am sure you have, even if the person did not explicitly say it to you.

Let's look at some example excerpts from typical greetings that we have all had at one time or another, and do some *judging* ourselves:

"Hello, you have reached Ted Auditor and I am either on the other line or away from my desk . . ."

Is that really necessary? Seriously, do we care if you are on the other line **or** if you are away from your desk? The second we hear your greeting, we know the deal; we get it, you are not available. In fact, many voicemail systems allow you to hit # to skip the message and just leave a voicemail right away, and that might be what we are doing right now.

*"Please leave me your name, your number, and the date and time in
which you called ..."*

Good intentions, but how many times have we heard that? Chances are
the message, which has good intentions, does not resonate anymore with
us. It's like the old Charlie Brown teacher: "Wah-wah-wah-wah." If we know
you well, we don't need that information anyway so it's not applicable most
of the time.

The date and time are retrievable on almost all voicemail systems already, and most of the time, auditors are robotic in checking their voicemail
several times during the day, so we'll know when you called anyway.

What Makes a Good Voicemail Greeting?

That is a subjective question of course.

Since this has always been a juicy subject when talking to auditors, here
are some considerations:

- *Try to be brief.* Try counting the number of words you use in your
  greeting. Remember that if a caller listens to the whole greeting, they
  also are lucky enough to hear the standard ending that annoys most
  of us and makes us wonder whether the cell phone companies are
  in collusion to make us spend more minutes on our cell phones: "To
  page this person, press 5 now. At the tone, please record your message.
  When you are finished recording you may press 1 for more options."
  By the way, many voicemail systems allow you to disable that feature.
  Do your callers a favor and do that. We'll all appreciate the brevity!
- *Be enthusiastic.* We'll probably remember your enthusiasm ahead of
  what you are actually saying. Remember you are selling yourself with
  your message. Convey enthusiasm, appreciation, and general happi-
  ness. Here is a tip: When you are having one of those great days in
  your life, create a new voicemail greeting then. Your pleasure will shine
  through and it will be real.
- *Tell us your name **clearly.***
- *Clear your throat before you record your greeting.* Be careful with the
  very beginning. We often hear someone inhale before they speak, but it
  would be better if you inhaled before you started recording the greeting.
  That inhale may set a negative tone (or just be kind of funny).
- *In some cases, your extension number might be useful, so tell us in your
  greeting what it is.* We mess up; we call the wrong number or extension
  occasionally. Also, sometimes we do not know what your extension is,
  and we had to go through your long name look-up feature from the
  main voicemail recording to just get your extension. If the system itself

does not inform the user of the extension (and you can easily check that), consider providing your extension with your greeting.

- *Try something subtle, professional, and creative!* You will be surprised about the number of comments you receive if you try something different. "This is Ted Auditor, please leave me a message." That is an example of a real simple greeting and if said enthusiastically, it might be all you need.
- *Listen to your voicemail on a different phone than the one you used to create it.* Volume levels differ, and background noise is not always apparent. Listen to how it sounds.

Your Brand

Are we sweating the details too much in talking about voicemails and voicemail greetings? Maybe, but all of that is part of selling yourself ... your brand.

The term *branding* means very little, most of the time, to young auditors. We chose to major in accounting instead of marketing for a reason!

But you are probably familiar with some of the best-known brands in the marketplace: Walmart, McDonald's, Apple, Microsoft, and so forth. You are familiar with them, but what do their brands represent to you? When you think of Microsoft and then Apple, you probably have two different sets of thoughts in your mind. Their marketing, their products, their customer service have all developed separate brands in your mind.

But what if we simplify the context of discussing the term *branding* around YOU. What is your brand? Visualize your name in lights, the letters of your name floating above your head. Now, as you see your name in lights, think about your name, who you are, and how you feel others perceive you. What comes to your mind? Whatever comes to your mind, **that is your brand.** You are a brand of one.

Your brand is affected by almost everything you do in life. When somebody who knows you describes your characteristics, **that is your brand.** When somebody assumes you will do something based on what they know of you, they have made an assumption based on their perception of your brand.

If you were to get a friend, colleague, or family member to choose words to describe you, they are describing your brand.

Uncover your brand, protect your brand, develop your brand, and most important, live your brand!

Following are some considerations on how to improve or protect your brand.

Be Responsive to People's Requests

How responsive are you to people? Your brand is developing in the minds of everyone you deal with on a daily basis. Do you return phone calls right away? Okay, maybe not right away, but do you return them in a reasonable amount of time consistently? Do you even return all the phone calls you should?

Think about certain vendors you work with in life, people such as lawyers, dentists, repairmen, and so on. How important is it that they respond to your questions, calls, or e-mails? Do you care that they might be busy servicing others? Not really. You care about your problem, and you want it solved. Their responsiveness is very important to you. That is, many times, the main reason you stay loyal to a certain vendor.

Every day, businesses are losing potential customers simply based on the inability of an individual to call someone back. Have you ever called a cable or phone company because you wanted to change service and nobody called you back? THEIR LOSS. Literally.

Make Each Person Feel He/She Is the Most Important Person in the World *When You Are with Them*

When someone is talking, resist the urge to interrupt. When they are talking, you should be listening, right? Sounds simple.

Can you think of another word that has all the same letters as the word L-I-S-T-E-N? Think about it for a while and, if you don't know, turn to the bottom of the next page.

If you are on the phone, answer with a great big hello. Smile throughout the call.

Buy a mirror; watch your face during a call if you have to ensure you are smiling. If possible, stand up and walk around, this physical act will automatically make you sound more enthusiastic.

Watch people who talk on their cell phones walking around one day. Compare that to someone talking on their phone sitting at their desk with papers piled up next to them. Generally, you will see a difference in their tone and enthusiasm. If you want to sound like you are enthusiastic and jumping out of your seat, then literally do that!

Start Them on a High

We have all heard that first impressions are important. Harry Beckwith in his book *What Clients Love* adds to this point when he says:

First impressions become self-fulfilling prophecies. We make immediate judgments about people, and then we fit everything we see to conform to our snap judgment.

When we form a bad first impression of someone, it can perpetuate throughout the relationship.

Does it go even further than that? Might we be self-fulfilling in OUR first impressions? Think back to when you made a great first impression with someone else. Did it perpetuate from there? Did you live up to your own highly set standard? Think about it the other way: When you made a bad first impression on someone and you knew it . . . did that taint how you felt about that relationship going forward? Did you live down to your own unfavorable first impression when dealing with that person going forward? Maybe.

First impressions are huge! Practice yours if you need to. Two questions to consider:

1. **What was interesting about your past weekend?** You know every-one's weekend is the main water-cooler topic come Monday morning. It's a common question even from people you do not know well or have just met. Take a few minutes to craft your answer. You will come across more clearly and enthusiastically to those who ask—and you know they will ask (more than one of them!).

2. **What do you do?** That can be a tough one, but not if you put some sincere thought into it and script it ahead of time. Some people call this your laser introduction or your business introduction. Some tips:
   - IF YOU WANT SOMEONE TO LEAVE YOU ALONE QUICKLY, JUST SAY YOU ARE AN AUDITOR IN AN UNENTHUSIASTIC WAY. THAT WILL WORK! They will run.
   - Think about your answer from the inquirer's point of view. People can relate more when you can articulate what you do in terms they understand.
   - Consider asking them a question as your lead. If you decide to do that, make SURE you listen to their answer. Don't make them feel like the question was so scripted that their answer does not really matter ... you are just ready to jump in again and finish answer-ing their question. Listen to their answer and continue listening and continue the conversation it starts. You can always come back to fully

Answer to question on page 17 = S-I-L-E-N-T.

answering their question. Sometimes it will be easy. Sometimes the conversation will be easy because you opened up for THEM.

Here are some examples. Remember, create an introduction that is authentic to you and that you would be comfortable saying. It must be natural. Sure, you can script it, but you do not want it to sound like a script when you say it.

Business Introduction Examples

Do you know any small business owners?

I help small companies grow by providing assurance and advisory services. I just recently was working with XYZ and we helped them to secure debt to grow their company ...

So how much do you know about what auditors do?

I work in an internal audit group at ABC company. I work specifically ...

Note: Remember, the lead question might be all you need!

Leave Them on a High

Consciously commit to ending all of your communications on a high note. How do people feel when they leave your office? Ask them if you are not sure. Feedback is important. If you are not convinced about this, turn to Chapter 3.

Sweat the Details

Spell check and grammar check your documents and e-mails, or ask someone else to do it. We really are picky as auditors. We do audit (and judge) everything! Have you ever spent a lot of time on a memo and asked for feedback only to first hear something about a misspelling or grammar error? We cannot resist. We are wordsmiths.

Have you ever had a great conversation with a person you just met only to realize that you called the person you were talking to by the wrong name? A person's name is far more than a "detail" ... Names matter, **big-time.** They'll remember your name snafu more than anything else you might have told them.

Be Consistent

If you tell somebody you will show up to a meeting, show up! If you tell someone you will have something done by 5:00 P.M. have a plan in place to have it to them by 5:00 P.M. at the very latest.

Also, be consistent in the way you approach and communicate with people. **Do you talk differently to an executive or partner versus a brand-new staff person?** You probably are thinking, "Of course I do!" We are not talking about what you say here; it's more that we've witnessed people who perk up, get enthusiastic, and put on their smiley face when the boss walks into the room, but act very differently when a younger staff person approaches. The boss knows he or she is important. The staff person should be treated equally in that regard. Staff want to be told they are important; sometimes they NEED to be told they are important, and your mannerisms, your enthusiasm, and your smiles do just that.

Here is one exercise to consider: During any one day, you probably talk to a lot of different people. You NEED to talk to some of these people, and you choose to talk to others. Is there consistency in the way that you talk to people? Let's assume someone magically recorded every single conversation you had during the day, the person you were talking to, the time, and not only what you said, but your tone as well. Then, magically, those conversations were typed into your own scrapbook. Now you are sitting on your couch and reviewing your daily conversations with those closest to you in your life, maybe your spouse, parents, siblings, and so on. How do your conversations come across to them? How do they come across to you? How do you WANT them to come across?

This exercise may be impossible. Maybe it's not. You could spend a few moments each day recording your thoughts on conversations you had with people.

The thing to consider is your ability to be reflective about your daily conversations and your ability to strive for consistency in them. You make the call on your own brand, deciding what equals your standards.

I know. Some of the conversations you hold are so brief, so fleeting that you do not see the value in even thinking about them. I challenge you not to underestimate your ability to have an influence on people around you, even in short encounters.

> It's the **little** details that are vital. **Little things** make **big things** happen.
>
> —*John Wooden*

It is very hard to always be "on" your game, to always be consistent in the manner you talk to people. Life happens. Challenges attack you.

Communication is not a science, it is an art. If you are different in your approach and communication to people based on their authority, if you are different in your approach and communication to people based on how you woke up that morning, a new word needs to be added to your brand: inconsistency.

If you are not responsive, if you don't sweat the details, if you are not consistent ... that is not necessarily right or wrong, but it does contribute to the brand being developed about you in other peoples' minds. The point is to consider what you want your brand to be and to realize all the things you do and say that contribute to it.

What Is the Difference between My Brand and My Values?

That is an important question to ponder. A brand is more about how others perceive you, how you come across to others, while your core values are the characteristics that are most important to you. A brand is made up of many things, how you introduce yourself, communicate, listen, and so on, while your values are the core convictions you hold dear to yourself and practice every day, even when nobody is around.

Maybe the specific question to ponder is: Do my core values come across to others, and do they enhance my brand?

Branding versus Selling

Who makes it to the top of the auditing world? Those who ATTRACT new business. That's not just for those working for professional service providers who can "sell" new auditing work; it's also for those who can "sell" new roles, new ideas, and leadership opportunities. How do YOU become most attractive? By continuously selling yourself and strengthening your brand. Others will want to work with you, and they will want to be around you.

Notice we did not talk once about selling services or marketing in this chapter. The title may have been deceiving. We chose not to discuss traditional service selling, because ...

If you can sell yourself every day in every encounter you have with others, that other selling will be easy.

As you grow in your career, you will be exposed to a lot more traditional selling tips, techniques, and processes. *There are a lot better books on that subject out there.*

BUT unless you can sell number one, the rest will not matter.

One other point: You have probably heard people say nobody can be "sold" and nobody wants to be sold to; people must choose to "buy." That is fair, and it makes this chapter seem kind of crazy in retrospect, because we have been using the word "sell" throughout it. Okay, turn it around, but many of the considerations will be the same: How are you branding yourself to lead people to want to "buy" from you?

So let's turn around the sentence before the preceding paragraph. **Unless others are attracted to you and want to "buy" the brand that is you, the rest will not matter.**

In the professional services industry, in the corporate world, and in the auditing world, people don't buy from companies, and in many cases they are not buying your product. They buy from people. They buy less-tangible services. They buy people. They buy **individual, well-branded people like you.**

Leadership Summary

How do you identify and develop your brand so that it feels very "expensive" and commands attention by everyone else because it is so apparent in everything you do?

LEAD by being aware that you are always selling yourself in everything that you do. You are always developing your brand in the minds of others. Uncover, protect, and live YOUR authentic brand. Sell yourself every day.

CHAPTER 3

Feedback Equals Money

I f you had to grade yourself and your organization on obtaining and using feedback, what grade would you give yourself? Your organization?

It's not as if we don't try. Yearly or semiannual written evaluations are usually forced upon us. Some of us occasionally provide informal feedback to those with whom we work, but we don't go nearly as far as we could.

Sources of Feedback

Ask yourself right now, how many people have you asked for feedback on YOUR performance in the past week?

Whom can we ask for feedback from?

- Professional colleagues
- Administrative staff
- Our boss(es)
- Direct reports
- Spouses, boyfriends, girlfriends, and other partners
- Clients
- Siblings
- Just about anybody!

What are some questions you can use to solicit feedback from various sources? Let's look at some below.

Keep in mind, some of the ideas below may go against company policy. For example, your firm may have a formal client feedback process with preprinted feedback questions.

However, if you are not already receiving answers to the PERSONAL questions below, consider asking them, or ones like them, yourself. **Be a rebel.**

Clients:

- Can you talk to me about your expectations of me in the role I hold in auditing your company?
- I get the sense you did not feel I handled that last situation in the best way I could have. How could I have handled that situation differently, so I can provide better personal service going forward? How can I specifically improve?
- How do you feel about our communication process? Do we talk enough during the year? Should I be more proactive in reaching out to you? When?
- What is your preferred method of communication: phone calls or e-mails?

Clients really like this question, because it is personal and it shows that you care about making your personal communication with them productive and efficient. In today's world there are so many ways to communicate: phone, voicemail, e-mail, texting, instant messaging (IM-ing), and so forth. Ask them for feedback on THEIR preferred method!

If you ask this question, record the answer wherever you store your contact information.

A partner once told me he preferred e-mail, but also that he was typically in the office every morning before 7:00 A.M. I capitalized on that very often; when I had some questions on which I wanted to talk to him directly, I called at 7:00 A.M., and my success rate was very high in reaching him. Now, when I open up his contact in Outlook, the first thing I see is his preferred communication methods and the best times to reach him live. That small piece of "feedback" saved me lots of time (and him as well)!

Staff, colleagues, peers, and so on:

- How could we have specifically managed that client better? I would love to get five ideas from you in an e-mail by Monday.
- We were not very efficient in auditing accounts receivable this year. What specific ideas do you have for doing a better job next time?
- What specific things did I do on this audit that made your life easier? What specific things made your life tougher?

Administrative staff:

- Are there any ways that we can work together in more efficient ways? Is there anything I do that you feel could be done a different way?
- Do I express my appreciation for how you support me enough?
- What are some ways I can make your job easier and simpler?

You understand these examples. You probably have better questions.

ASK THEM. ASK THEM OFTEN. SEE HOW PEOPLE REACT.

Just by asking, you are delivering a message ... a message that is uplifting and simple ... *you value their feedback, and if you value their feedback, you value THEM*. You are smart enough to know that your own learning curve is going to SPEED UP DRAMATICALLY if you can use the feedback of others.

Do you know what else it says? It says that you realize we are all in this together. It says that you realize that success for both of you is interdependent. It says you care about the relationship and want to be intentional about improving it.

I am the type of guy who survives on constant feedback.

—Jon Gruden

(second youngest NFL football coach ever to win a Super Bowl)

Performance Evaluations

It is September 28. You have 58 hours to write and complete four performance evaluations. You have procrastinated for weeks on these things. You really do not enjoy doing them. Ahhhh, what the heck, let's wait until tomorrow night to get these done!

Why do many people hate doing performance evaluations? Some answers we have heard include:

- They take too long.
- They never do any good or help improve performance.
- The forms themselves are cumbersome and restrictive.
- They force us to write negative things, and that is no fun.
- They are just an administrative issue, and they have nothing to do with the important part of our job, serving clients!

What about a different perspective, a different reason?

Could the reason we hate doing performance evaluations be ...

... that we *stink* at doing performance evaluations?

They take a long time because, often, we are starting with a completely blank piece of paper. We have all been there. It probably does not say in your job descriptions something about excelling in completing written performance evaluations. But these are a vehicle for feedback and improvement, and career development, so they are important.

And there is an EASIER way.

Here is a tip: When you are in a bind and trying to do a performance evaluation, get others to do a lot of it for you! That's right ... get feedback on the person you are evaluating from the other people with whom they work, even clients. Tell them, "I am preparing Ted Auditor's performance evaluation and I value your feedback." They don't even have to be people who worked on a job recently with that person, just people who might be able to provide feedback on the person.

What they say may spark a memory of something that person did while working with you. Sometimes, they will have great details, too, and specific stories to tell about the person. They will provide you with insights you may not have recalled or planned to mention. They may also provide you with more support for items you were going to bring up already. This approach should be standard, but sometimes we forget. The benefits are numerous: It makes it easier on you, it provides different perspectives, and it provides different sources, stories, and examples to back up the points you wish to make.

Another tip would be to continually capture items of feedback for that person's performance review. Create a "people tracker" folder on your computer, possibly including a Word document for every person with whom you work frequently at your firm. If there is a story or example you want to capture, put it in there for future use.

Now, of course, you are probably saying to yourself, *I already do that. I just don't track it. I continually provide feedback to my staff orally.* **That is great.** Not enough of us do that. If you do that consistently, then the formal performance evaluation will be no surprise to the recipient. Great! We'd still encourage you to capture it though, because (1) it will still be easier to write the formal feedback at the end, and (2) a people-tracker document can help you track someone's progress on a long-term basis. How cool would it be to revisit a people tracker and see that you targeted certain areas for improvement a while back, and now that person is flourishing in those areas? How rewarding would it be to be able to specifically mention past examples (even several months ago) where they struggled, while mentioning current examples where they have demonstrated growth? Do you think they will remember your feedback? Your feedback is now going beyond just little things, it is pointing out GROWTH.

All important feedback you capture in your people tracker should of course be communicated as soon as needed, which is usually immediately.

This may make the formal review somewhat boring. Most of it will be repetition of what you have already communicated. That is great. **Use the extra time for what is most valuable**—helping your colleagues create specific, measurable action steps and accountability methods to improve their professional development.

Without feedback, we don't know the areas in which we excel or require improvement. With feedback, we can focus on such areas. We can improve, which in turn creates better professionals, resulting in better-served clients, higher realization rates, superior mentoring and coaching to colleagues, and better relationships!

In short, the ability to solicit and use feedback represents dollars to those who excel at it. FEEDBACK EQUALS MONEY.

Feedback Is Contagious

Every time you relay feedback to a colleague, you are providing them value. The feedback may be positive, or it may have an eye toward improvement. If communicated in a positive way, the receiver will notice your gesture and, in many cases, will want to reciprocate. This approach destroys barriers of negative competitiveness. It creates an atmosphere of continuous improvement and humility. **All of a sudden, YOU have started a feedback culture.**

Of course there is a major caveat to this theory. If the feedback is totally self-serving and does not have the interest of the other at heart, it does not fulfill your purpose: improvement.

Let's say you are in your car one morning. You are cranky from a lack of sleep. You are late to work. Your sports team blew a big lead last night. **You are downright nasty.** Providing feedback in the form of a one-fingered gesture to the car in front of you who is not going as fast as you feel they should is not what we're talking about. That kind of feedback might give you some temporary venting relief (it will not help you feel better in the long run), but it's not what we are talking about here. Valuable feedback, whether it is positive or constructive, comes from someone who is trying to help the other person, the team, and the company improve.

This might sound obvious, but it is not always obvious in practice. Human beings are infinitely more emotional than we are logical. Have you ever felt the need to simply tell someone off about some issue that had you frustrated? Recount what you said, or wanted to say. It probably did not include constructive feedback—the kind of feedback that would provide value to the other person and help improve the situation. It probably was an emotional venting, much like the one-fingered example. Before you give someone feedback, take a step back for a moment and ask yourself how that feedback is going to provide value to the other person and help solve the challenge you are facing (versus simply helping you to feel temporarily better emotionally). This practice will, in some cases, have you totally changing your approach to providing the feedback or, in some cases, cause you to cease giving it all together!

If you feel the need to provide negative feedback, and your emotions are REALLY getting the best of you, read Chapter 17.

Remember to ask yourself, "What is the intent of my feedback in this situation?"

Is it just to feel better about yourself, or is it meant to make the current situation or a working relationship better? If it is just to make you feel better, then provide it to someone else, someone you can trust. Really, all you need here is an outlet to vent.

If it is the latter, again ask yourself a question: Is the method I am about to use to provide feedback the best way to get to the desired result: improvement?

Specific Feedback Rocks!

Be as specific as possible with all feedback, including positive feedback.

"You did a great job in auditing cash," can be replaced with, "I liked the approach you took in auditing cash. I specifically liked your testing of the reconciliation, including your documentation of the related controls and how that affected your approach. I am going to make a copy of that work paper and share that with some of my other staff."

Relay positive feedback! Find creative ways to provide positive feedback! Do it when it's not expected, such as via voicemail, in front of other people (if you know they would enjoy public recognition), at random times of the day, and so forth. Some samples of positive feedback follow.

- "Jim was talking about you behind your back. He said you did a great job on your last audit, especially with your write-up of the deferred revenue issue. I asked him for that memo, and I am going to use part of it as a template for another client because it was written so well."
- "The client commended you yesterday on your attitude, saying you had good 'tongue biting skills' in working with Joe, the payroll person."
- On a voicemail: "Hi Ted, it's Suzy; it's late and I am still here trying to finish up the XYZ audit. This has been a really tough audit for all of us, but I wanted to say thanks for all your hard work. If it wasn't for you, I'd be sleeping here tonight. Thanks again!"
- "Do you know what a positive impact you are having on Jim's career? You have been a great role model for him. He always talks about how he enjoys working on your jobs, and how you take time out to ensure he not only understands how to get the auditing procedures accomplished, but also why they are important. We all know we should do this, and many of us know in the long run that practice actually saves us time, but few of us proactively do this with our staff. Can you tell me ... WHAT IS YOUR SECRET?"

A Feedback Culture Can Start with You

In the last 10 years, the term *360 degrees of feedback* has become a buzz phrase.

Some CPA firms, internal audit departments, and other audit shops may be excelling in this area, but many firms who have such a program, where the notion of providing upward feedback is a formal part of the firm's evaluation process, still struggle with it in practice. First, when it's forced by a formal process, it sometimes lacks the honesty needed. Second, it's just not always easy to give feedback to your boss, even if it is anonymous. Many times that has nothing to do with the effectiveness of the feedback process; it's more about the openness to feedback of the person you are evaluating.

The way you change that is by starting with yourself.

Possibly the most underutilized source of feedback in the accounting industry is the staff who work under you. If you are a senior, you should be tapping that resource weekly, if not daily. If you are a manager, get all your seniors together for lunch one day and ask them how you could improve as a manager. And OF COURSE executives and partners should do the same thing. It takes a lot of humility to do this, but it demonstrates a lot of strength at the same time.

You will get great feedback, and you will **INSTANTLY** improve the morale at your firm. Those who work under you will feel valued, and a crazy thing will happen ... **it will become contagious.**

Now I know one thing you are thinking: *Some people will never go for this. They have never asked for feedback. They don't want feedback. They are above me on the food chain and they don't see the real need.*

Those are usually the same people who resist change. This scenario is a great **challenge** for you!

Does everyone resist change?
The question is: Do people resist change or do people resist *BEING CHANGED*?

Spite them in a positive way: **Ask *them* for feedback.** Encourage others at your firm to ask them for feedback. First off, you may be surprised about the value of what they provide you. Because they are perceived as people who are stubborn and would never want feedback themselves, people have probably never asked them for feedback in the past, so this might open a new window for them. Second, as we said, this stuff can be contagious. Who knows what effect it will have on them until you try it?

People enjoy providing feedback. Most people are not solicited enough for their feedback. It's not about those long feedback forms either. Those might be great tools, but the most value may be gained in obtaining feedback face-to-face. Look people straight in the eyes. Asking them for advice on how you can get better at what you do and in working with them can be a very powerful exercise. Can't find the time to do it? In our virtual world, there is nothing wrong with asking for feedback in an e-mail, text message, or IM. We live in a fast-paced world, and your feedback will need to be fast-paced in some cases. Think about it this way: Do you know anyone who complains about getting TOO much feedback at his or her job? Do you know anyone who left an organization because he or she was receiving too much feedback?

Providing feedback makes people feel important, especially if you are higher on the perceived food chain (organizational chart) than they are.

They'll surprise you, too.

Don't make assumptions. Be that rebel. Start with yourself. Grab as much "money" (feedback) as you can, and pass it around to others. Soon everyone is richer for it.

Tips for good feedback:

- *Specific*—General feedback is better than nothing, but specific feedback with good examples is desirable because it provides context, it provides clear evidence, and it is much more memorable.
- *Actionable*—Ask yourself, what can they specifically do with this feedback? Sometimes we forget that when we are providing positive, constructive feedback to someone, we want to encourage them to simply continue that behavior. What is the specific call to action you want to encourage with your feedback?
- *Measurable*—The actions that are part of the feedback should be measurable, so the recipient knows he or she is making progress toward goals. Examples of measures include:
  - *Length of time*—For example, "Complete this action within six weeks."
  - *Deliverables*—For example, "Write an article for publication."
  - *Counts*—For example, "Provide feedback to your team members ONCE per week."
- *Emotional*—Ask yourself: Does this feedback appeal to a person's sense of self-worth? We have been told for years that we should not express emotion in the office. Hogwash! We are emotional people. There is nothing wrong with showing a little emotion once in a while. It shows your passion for success, and showing a little emotion in providing feedback shows your passion for OTHERS' SUCCESS.

- *Team-oriented*—Good feedback is not made in a vacuum where the only perceived benefit is to you, or to the one person you are targeting. Focus on how others can benefit, and how your organization can benefit. Show them how, by doing these things, they are becoming a leader!
- *Depersonalized*—Focus on actions, not on people. If you are going to bring emotion into it, make sure your emotion is about values and actions, not about personalities and people.

> If you manage others effectively, you likely have a style of giving feedback that leaves people feeling challenged rather than threatened.
>
> —*Jim Loehr*, The Power of Full Engagement

- *Accountable*—The feedback that you are providing, the actions that should be taken in response—you should demonstrate not only how they are measurable, but also how the person can be held accountable for taking steps to continue certain behavior and improve it. Do they need help in holding themselves accountable? That does not mean you have to hold their hand; it simply means you care about their growth and helping them achieve the necessary steps for improvement. We have all been through feedback sessions where the other person nods their head at everything you say, yet you still have some reservations about whether you made your points well and whether they really heard you. In every case, try not to tell them how to do something. Tell them what needs to happen, and ask THEM how they feel they should get it done. This creates early buy-in from them. It is easy and sometimes natural to rebel against someone's feedback when they are telling you what needs to change. It will be much more effective when the person receiving the feedback sees the need and helps to create the action plan.

Gen Y professionals (those born between 1977 and 1988), sometimes also referred to as the IM generation, crave continuous feedback. They want to know instantly when they have done something well, and they want to know instantly how you can help them improve their skills if they did something poorly. They are not accustomed to our historical yearly means of providing feedback. They need it as fast as they work.

Leadership Summary

Use feedback to take your leadership skills to the next level:

- Exhaust all sources of feedback to you; they will help you learn new things about yourself and about those around you. You will show others that you VALUE their feedback and open up communication lines for mutual improvement.
- Be specific and consistent in your feedback to others in performance evaluations ... and all the time!
- Start with yourself. Help kindle a culture of feedback by requesting it and providing it, with an eye toward positive improvement.

"No organizational action has more power for motivating employee behavior change than feedback from credible work associates."
—Mark R. Edwards

CHAPTER 4

The Audit Cheerleader

Statistics from both Major League Baseball and the National Football League prove what most fans already know: A home team generally enjoys an advantage over a road team. You can probably think of a number of different reasons why this might be the case. Some factors may include the road team having to travel before the game, the home team being familiar with the surroundings and field, or the impact of the fans and their support on the game.

If a home team enjoys an advantage in sports, the question is, how can you create a "home team" atmosphere to lead your colleagues and teams to take their "game" to the next level? No matter what level you are, you have a major opportunity to contribute to the friendly atmosphere *your* home team enjoys.

Belief Is Mandatory

Cheerleaders do it. Die-hard fans do it. Team leaders do it. If you have ever been part of a sports team that was very successful, you know one of the reasons why: Everyone believed in the ability of the team to accomplish its goals.

How many audits have you been a part of where the team spends some real time thinking about what desired results looks like, even going as far as visualizing those results?

How do you build belief? Ask your team:

- How do we win? Let's define success, both as a team and individually.
- What are the important roles we will all have to help the team achieve our goals?
- How will we overcome the roadblocks that will invariably appear?
- How do we support each other in times of crisis and triumph?

- How will we tackle conflict, both among our group and with the client?
- How do (will) we celebrate achievement of our goals?

Think about the person or people in your life who you would describe as a positive mentor. What characteristics did that person, or those people, have?

One of the most important things they probably did was BELIEVE in you. They sought to build up your confidence and your competence. You probably do not remember them harping on your deficiencies but, rather, pointing out your strengths and your potential. They went out of their way to show you and express to you that you were going to be successful. By simply believing in people, we build them up and we help them maximize their potential.

Conversely, if you want to limit a person's potential, if you want to slow down their growth, the best way to do that is by consistently pointing out their blunders, their mistakes, and the ways they could have done things better. If you believe your "players" and your team will fail, if you do not believe it can be done, then you will almost always be correct. They will live down to your belief. You will have a better chance of failing, and so will your team! Auditors in particular are good at uncovering weaknesses. We are paid to do that in reviews of operations, internal controls, financial statement reporting, and a host of other areas. Be wary of taking that too far in leading others. Do we need to know about weaknesses? Yes, but belaboring them only brings someone down. If you are going to belabor anything, belabor your belief in them to work on their weaknesses.

The opposite of building belief is building fear, and many of us are guilty of that.

- "If we do not get this report done soon, the entire audit will be in danger."
- "You did not get that done last time! What makes you so sure you can do it now?"
- "There is no way the client will deliver on time!"
- "We must have the open items completed by Friday, or we are in trouble."
- "I do not see how we have enough time to get all of this done. This is ridiculous!"

All of these statements express disbelief and fear. Some people motivate by fear, some people motivate by encouragement, and a lot of us do both. Regardless of which tactic is more effective, ask yourself: Which way do you want to manage and lead?

What if you do not believe in your team's ability to accomplish the task at hand? It does not matter if you are the highest-level employee or the lowest-level, you need to be on board with the "belief" factor. Ask yourself WHAT NEEDS TO HAPPEN for you to believe in the team and make those things happen, because if you don't, you are making it tough for yourself (and the team) from the beginning. What resources do we need? Whose buy-in do we need? Don't just ask yourself these questions, ask the team. What do we need to be able to believe in ourselves here? Most of it is on you and the team, but you do not want lack of resources to be a reason for nonbelief. If lack of resources is a reason for nonbelief, you want to be able to dispel that notion before you get started. How do we accomplish our goals in light of a perceived lack of resources? Whatever it takes.

How do you communicate belief? Easily. You tell a person you believe in them, or sometimes better yet, you tell others. For example, if you have a staff auditor who is about to lead his or her first audit engagement, send an e-mail to everyone on the team and tell them about your belief in that person's ability to do a great job. Let that belief permeate throughout the team, and it will. When someone shows strong belief in you before you do something, like most people, you will fight hard to live up to that belief.

The Shawshank Redemption, released in 1994, was a gripping movie, the story of Andy Dufresne's escape from the fictional Shawshank State Prison. Andy (played by Tim Robbins), an accountant, was wrongly imprisoned for murdering his wife. His survival in that prison in the face of horrible adversity, and his subsequent escape, were elaborate and miraculous. But as inspiring as Andy's escape in the movie was, there is much more to the story and movie.

There were two other characters, among others, of note: Brooks Hatlen, known as simply "Brooks," and Ellis Redding, known as "Red" (played brilliantly by Morgan Freeman).

Brooks was finally granted parole after living in Shawshank for more than half his life. Brooks, after getting out and securing a job as a grocery clerk, soon took his own life after failing to find little respect or any kind of meaningful role on the outside. He did not want to be released from Shawshank, and he even tried to commit a crime after he found out about his impending release, so he might stay, stay in a place where he felt important in his role as a librarian in the prison.

Red was granted release many years later, and he too found a job as a grocery clerk, in the same store no less. He too struggled with being in the outside world, because freedom was actually uncomfortable for him. He lived in the same hotel as Brooks did for a while, the same place that Brooks hung himself.

Why did Red choose not to do the same as Brooks? Why did he choose to "get busy livin' " instead of "get busy dyin' "? It was simple. Andy believed in Red. He STRONGLY believed in him and told him as much before his escape. He told him he would need him and his skills once he was granted release, and his role would be important, and HE WAS IMPORTANT.

The last two words spoken in the movie, by Red, as the credits are about to come streaming down, are "I believe," but if there could have been a caption above, it might have read, "Somebody believed in me."

The final question here is not who you believe in, but WHO KNOWS YOU BELIEVE IN THEM?

Conflict Is Healthy

Conflict typically represents opportunity—an opportunity for a resolution, an opportunity for a stronger team, and an opportunity for those involved to grow as a result.

Try thinking about conflict that way: Conflict = opportunity. See conflicts as solutions opportunities. Be a possibility thinker.

One of the biggest opportunities to lead when dealing with conflict is to depersonalize it. People don't do that enough. They take disagreements personally. I have seen this over and over when working with auditors. "He said" or "she said" comes up a lot. We look to be correct more than we look for the best way to handle an issue. We audit each other, on a personal level, too much. The personal conflict actually takes over the solution process.

"You told me you would have that section of the audit done by Monday, and now it is not done and you have to roll off this job. You should have finished your work, or, at a minimum, you should have given me more advance notice that you would not be able to complete it. You have just set back our entire audit plan."

There is a problem that needs addressing here but the "you," "you," "you," "you" does not help the situation. It places personal blame and has little to do with solving the problem. It fosters personal conflict. The person on the other end of this is going to feel like you are calling him or her incompetent; that person's ego is going to be hurt, and he or she will probably fight back hard or withdraw in a way that will make it difficult to talk to them at all. Remember: It is the actions and results you are unhappy with, not the person. Whether this becomes a training opportunity or is just a motivational issue, the effectiveness of your communication and the person's input into coming up with the best next actions is going to be enhanced if you can focus on what needs to be done now and in the future, not harping on what the person did wrong. That needs to be communicated, sure, but think about the best way to do that so a solution can be created.

- *Provide a summary of what went wrong.* Consider getting the person's input on the situation first. Maybe there is more to what happened than you think. If there is a good reason the work did not get done, even a hardship that caused the situation . . . be empathetic. But also keep your eye on the need for improvement, both the person's improvement and the team's! Always remember, there is a MAJOR difference between talking about something that "went wrong" and trying to prove someone was wrong.

Consider asking the person if there is anything you could have done to contribute to a different outcome. Again, this helps to depersonalize the conflict. Instead of seeing it as "me versus you" or "I told you so!" you are presenting the feedback as "us" reflecting on the situation together and both taking ownership for it.

- *Link their actions to the overall negative impact.* In the example above, maybe the impact is that now you must work crazy hours to catch up based on their incomplete work, or maybe it is an unsatisfied client. Be specific. Take it as far as you can: "You have to work late." What does that mean? (Maybe they have been working late a lot lately.) "The client is unsatisfied." What does that mean? Most of us have been through a feedback session where someone points out perceived flaws but there is little evidence of negative impact; it just seems like someone is being nitpicky. That feels personal. If you link the actions to negative impact and go very far with the negative impact, they will know WHY it is such a big deal and why changes and actions need to be developed. It helps depersonalize the situation because it is what it is. The results, which have been clarified, are unacceptable, not the person. Big difference.
- *Figure out next steps.* Ask them what can be done now. Sure, there are times where you just have to tell them exactly what needs to be done. Maybe there is a time famine, the next steps are obvious, and getting started is important. Or the person may have no idea what to do and may be just trying to turn a problem over to you. Or the person wants to just be provided with the answer to the next step. However, there can be some real development opportunities in putting the onus on the person to come up with solutions to the problem. First, it helps to push the ownership to that person, which is where it should be. Second, the person may have some really good ideas, but those ideas will most likely only come through if he or she trusts that you are more concerned with rectifying the situation than placing blame and guilt on his or her shoulders. The person is probably already feeling bad about the situation. If you force-feed the solution, the person does not feel like he or she is part of the solution; he/she was just the culprit and now you have come in to fix the situation. The person has failed in his or her own eyes. If you offer the chance to help fix the problem, you have given the person an opportunity to salvage his or her pride, something not many auditor leaders do. Reinforce the importance of that, too. Tell the person you expect that from now on, when presenting situations like

this, that he or she will have already come up with ideas for next steps and possible solutions. That will foster growth and minimize conflict.

- *End the conversation in a positive way.* If you have them feeling really bad about what happened, how does that lead to improved performance going forward? Consider expressing to them how this can end up in a very good way. Leave them with some belief in their ability to grow from the situation. Ask them how you can support them going forward.

Personalized conflict is not healthy. It makes people feel like they have to win; they must win for themselves. They must save their ego and their pride. When conflict turns into a competition to save ego, then the opportunity for action to improve the situation gets lost in a maze of trying to save pride. Have you ever been in an argument that digressed to more than just the original conflict? Here is an example to illustrate this. You are working with a staff auditor. A copy of an agreement has been misplaced, it's important, and you are down to the wire in trying to get an audit completed. You are sure the staff auditor lost it and you are upset. The staff auditor is sure he or she gave it to you and you lost it. Getting a replacement copy at this time is not an easy thing. This kind of conflict can go down a path to nowhere. These conversations can digress into a situation in which proving who is right and who is wrong is such a big deal that discrediting the other person becomes an agenda item. Some people will bring up past events in which things were lost—"Since I can remember and prove you have lost items in the past, it must be very possible you did the same thing again. You ARE the literal 'loser' here, and I can prove it, and thus I can win our personalized argument. I win. You lose."

Think about it this way: When that agreement is finally found, and it is either with your stuff or the staff auditor's stuff, will that be a "victory" for one over the other? If that is the case, then the teamwork aspect is hurt; the whole will not be stronger than the sum of the parts, because teams do not have teammates defeating teammates, they have common goals and they support each other throughout. In this case, it's all about finding the document, not placing blame. Be careful to discern between the goal of winning an argument (which is usually about your agenda) and the goal of solving the problem that created the conflict. There is a big difference.

Depersonalized conflict is healthy. It creates an environment where a TEAM is looking for resolutions, not INDIVIDUALS on opposing sides looking to win an argument.

So how do we depersonalize conflict? You focus on the situation, ideas, and results. You don't focus on the *who* as much as you do the *what* and the *how*. You do not focus on one person or the other being right, but on the team coming up with the best solution going forward. Following are some questions to answer when you feel like conflict is getting personal or becoming too negative.

What Is the Problem?

Make sure the problem is stated and clear and that everyone is on the same page. Instead of stating it yourself, you might want to have the other person(s) state it. Using our example above, one could say, "So talk to me about the situation we have with us getting the work completed and your schedule." That will help you AVOID conflict in many cases, because now you are seeking to uncover the issue and you are doing it by first learning their perspective.

If you are already embroiled in a state of conflict, see if you cannot have both parties step back and ensure that the problem has been defined. "Why are we arguing?" Sometimes the best question to answer is "What are we trying to accomplish by arguing?"

How Do You Restate the Problem or Root of the Conflict as an Opportunity?

A problem well stated is a problem half solved.
—Charles Kettering

This is a tough one. It takes an optimist. It takes a real CheerLEADER. It is difficult to always be optimistic while facing conflict, but this is where you need to be reflective about how much of a leader you want to be. It's too easy to get down in the face of conflict; it's too easy to let it become emotionally draining. It takes a lot of courage to see problems and conflict as opportunities. If we never had conflict, we would not be able to grow. Life is going to throw conflict at you; that is inevitable. You can only control the way you react to that conflict. Turning conflict into an opportunity for growth is a leader's perspective. The leader sees depersonalized conflict as healthy, as a WAY TO LEARN from another person. Dudley Field Malone once said, "I have never in my life learned anything from any man who agreed with me." Make sure you filter out what is trying to be accomplished. Disagreement is healthy—maybe even healthy enough that you can welcome it as a way to GET WHAT YOU NEED ACCOMPLISHED. The resolution represents the opportunity, and the conflict and disagreement are part of the path to getting there.

Honest disagreement is often a good sign of progress.
—Mohandas K. Gandhi

If you have ever been a die-hard fan of a sports team, you have probably experienced the high that can come from a big victory and the low that can come from a big defeat. It is pretty easy to be a big fan when things are going really well for your team. Conversely, it can be tough when your team has a terrible game or a terrible year. That is when your true "fandom" is tested, and in many cases, fans will abandon a team and not support them as much when they are losing. So, the question is, are they fans of the team, or are they just fans of the team when the going is good? Likewise it is easy to be supportive of your colleagues when everything is hunky-dory. It is in those tough moments, when it is difficult to be positive, that the true opportunity for real leadership lies. It takes a real leader to see problems as opportunities. The challenge is not only for you to see that, but for you to lead others to do the same thing.

So when you are facing conflict with one person, restate that as an opportunity to learn from that person and for the two of you to grow. Try it with a team as well. Conflict represents opportunity. When everyone takes the time to step back from the emotions of conflict and see it as an opportunity for ALL involved to grow, and to express it that way, you will instantly notice a change from the other persons involved. Now, instead of competition for who might be right and wrong, it is a quest for solutions. It is an opportunity because you presented it that way. Everyone sees it that way.

One last point on conflict: Once you have resolved it in a positive way, remind those involved that what started out as conflict is now going to end up as growth, for both/all of you! Auditors do not do that enough! That recognition is noteworthy, because it will convey the notion to the team that you do not shy away from conflict and they shouldn't either. Your team will be stronger with that attitude going forward. They will be individually stronger, too, and may not shy away from conflict as much, especially with you. Hmmmm, sounds like some respect building! Maybe conflict is healthy?

Positivity Is Contagious

The world of auditing is not stress-free. It is not without controversy, challenges, tough deadlines, and surprises. Those things are inevitable. Any team, sports-related or not, will have similar challenges to overcome, and one of the most important characteristics to help you to overcome the challenges is a positive attitude. Sounds simple, doesn't it?

What is not simple is continuously challenging yourself to ask whether you are contributing to a positive or negative environment via your attitude and actions.

To create a winning environment, a real home-field advantage, consider the following:

- Praise your colleagues whenever possible. Be specific in your praise. Delight in their progress. Reflect on their personal growth and how far they have come.
- Remind your fellow colleagues about how important their roles are in the big picture.
- Remind your fellow colleagues about past successes, the team's successes, their personal successes, and what they did specifically.
- Appreciate your organization out loud. Look for all the good things in your company and remind people of them.
- Talk a lot about how good it is going to feel when you and your team overcome your challenges.

BUILD confidence! Build people up not only to their face, but in front of others. That can be a mighty reinforcement tool. They did something positive, and you tell the world. Don't discriminate. Sometimes we feel like praise is meant for those people who work "under" us. It is for everyone. Sincere praise is welcomed by everyone! Seeing a staff auditor praise an executive in a specific genuine way is a real sign of leadership. Seeing an executive or partner praise a staff auditor is also enlightening.

The other great thing about doing this . . . It reinforces a behavior that others might pick up on and duplicate. You are telling others about positive deeds, and they might start doing the same for their colleagues. They might start doing it for you! One of the biggest ways you can create a home-field advantage with your colleagues is through the simple act of showing your folks that you are behind them, you appreciate them, and you support them, both as individuals and as part of the team.

Conversely, if you want to bring down the team, if you want to take away the home-field advantage, make sure you do the following things. We have ALL done these before:

- Complain about clients and colleagues behind their back.
- Blame others for any negative event. Defer responsibility whenever you can.
- Talk about how tough the challenges are that are facing you and your team. Talk about how demoralizing they are, and how impossible they will be to overcome. Talk about how badly things can go and what can happen if you do not achieve your goals.
- Complain about not having enough time or other resources to get anything done.

■ Get together at a happy hour and talk about all your problems and the organization's problems. Laugh with each other about it. Pile on.

Have you ever been involved in a powwow where you and some colleagues were discussing shortcomings of another auditor? Maybe it was in the office or at an audit site, or maybe it was at a happy hour? Many of us have. Sometimes you feel some kind of bonding in this activity.

"Can you believe what Sally Auditor was wearing yesterday?" "I know what you mean; what was she thinking?"

"Can you believe how Ted Auditor blames everyone but himself for not getting his work done?"

While it might seem fun at times, and you might feel some short-term satisfaction in getting others to agree with your thoughts, what kind of message does it deliver? First, it tells people that you are willing to talk about others in negative ways behind their back. The very people you are talking and bonding with will eventually deduct that you can do that to anyone, including them. This behavior hurts trust levels. Second, it creates a negative atmosphere. The more negative thoughts you communicate to others, the more likely for them to do the same to you, and now you are contagious. That demoralizes those around you. Many individuals do not realize the multiplier effect of a bad mood or of talking negatively about others. It expends negative energy. It demoralizes you. You'll probably agree that you are most productive when you are highly motivated and energized, so it makes sense that you will fall short of your potential on days when you are not as highly motivated and energized. Which activity is going to make you more motivated and energized—talking negatively about your situation and about others, or trying to see the positives?

Are you a builder or a breaker? If you want to be known as a builder, build up everyone else! Next time, in your powwow with other colleagues, think about ways you can talk positively about those not in the room. Not only will you have a positive influence on those people, but you will have it on yourself. Have you ever regretted talking positively about someone? On the other hand, have you ever regretted or reflected on a conversation you had in the past where you talked ill of another? If it is the latter, then the regret is probably not just what you said, but the feeling you have about yourself because you chose to say it. The reverse is true, as well. When you start talking about others in positive ways, you will start thinking about yourself in positive ways!

How do you remain optimistic and positive, especially during tough days and times? You do it intentionally. You take a look at yourself in the mirror. You ask yourself questions like: What are the methods I can use to ensure I am at my best in terms of my positive attitude? What are the ideas I can implement, on a daily basis if needed, that will help me have the most positive attitude possible during my day? Following are some ideas.

Identify Potential Inspiration or Motivation Routines

Think about the things you do that get you fired up. Is it having an intense workout? Running? Listening to music you really enjoy? What books, movies, blogs, articles, speeches, or quotes get you going? You may choose to use one of these every day. For example, you find that running three miles every morning gets you ready to tackle the day. Make a list of resources like this to draw on when the going gets tough. If you are down one morning, or have a tough day ahead of you, pull up your list of motivational resources and make a choice to do one of them at that time. The key is to be reflective about these kinds of things. Different people will have totally different methods and ideas in this area. That is great. Maybe you have a special memento you have saved, a card one of your kids made for you or a letter that was written to you that means something. Take it out and spend some time reflecting on it. That can be one of your inspiration routines! So dancing to hip-hop music right before you take the CPA exam might not be your idea of inspiration, but what will it be for the all-important meeting you are about to hold next week? Is there something you can do that will have you floating in a sea of positivity before you hold it?

Once you become better at doing this with yourself, try doing it with others. What subjects do people enjoy discussing? How are those around you motivated? Is it the thrill of overcoming a challenge? It is working together as a team? Is it recognition of a job well done? If you want to be a leader, you need to lead individuals, and to do that, you must treat them individually by understanding them individually. Once you have a feel for what motivates them, you can do a better job of motivating them. Which leads to the next question: What are your motivation routines for motivating those around you?

Mark Twain once said, "The best way to cheer yourself up is to cheer everyone else up." So next time you are down, really down about something, and you are looking to brighten up your thoughts and attitude, think about others. Try mailing out some thank-you cards (find a reason!), surprise someone with a gift, or dish out some unsolicited praise to those around you. Try it and see how you feel. See if it doesn't get your juices flowing a little bit. Maybe consider acting downright weird and telling that person, also. "I was kind of down this morning and I thought buying you a small gift would life my spirits. It did. Here it is." That is definitely weird!

Surround Yourself with Positive Influences

You have probably heard the old expression "birds of a feather flock together." If your goal is to be more generally positive, then surround yourself with people who are either naturally positive, in your opinion, or those who have a similar goal. Spend some time running through your list of friends and associates and identify those who bring a smile to your face because they exude positivity. They do not have to be accountants. Spend (more) time with them. Consider making it a routine, maybe a monthly lunch. Tell them the reason you want to do this. They will be flattered.

Remember Your Successes

Conjure up memories of times when you faced challenges and overcame them. Why were you successful? How did you overcome the barriers to success? How can you learn from that now? What were your critical success factors? How did your attitude come into play? You will learn from it; it might remind you about your own resolve, and it *will* remind you of success and help motivate you to repeat it.

One opportunity in this area is to *be specific* about your past successes. What was it about the environment that helped foster your success? Can those factors be replicated?

Appreciate What You Have

The act of appreciation can inspire positivity. How many things can you think of in your life that make you feel appreciative? How many people in your life make you feel thankful? Consider documenting some of the things you appreciate about your life. Maybe an appreciation journal? Document your appreciation daily or weekly. The act of expressing appreciation, even if it is just to yourself, will get you in a mood of seeing the better things in life. It also may put certain current circumstances into perspective.

Explicitly expressing appreciation can be contagious, and maybe it is as good for the giver as it is for the receiver. If you choose to do an appreciation inventory more often, you may find yourself wanting to express such newly uncovered appreciation more often to those people around you.

> People who express appreciation for what they have attract people who recognize that attitude. They are far more inclined to encourage and/or lend a helping hand because they know their help will be appreciated.
>
> —*Zig Ziglar*

Track Your Positivity Progress

Consider reflecting on your days and how your attitude changed or improved or digressed. Ask people for feedback if it's something you really feel strongly about improving. Some questions you could ask:

- Is my attitude positive or negative, in your opinion?
- Do you feel uncomfortable informing me of bad news, based on how you feel I will respond? How do I respond to bad news? Do I make you feel better about the situation, just the same, or worse? How could I get better at that?
- How would you describe me in terms of how positive a person I am? Do you have any examples to help me see that? Do you have any tips for me?

Remember from Chapter 3 that you can gain valuable insights from many sources when soliciting feedback. It's sometimes hard for us to always see or be aware of our own attitude. We may think we have good intentions, but no one else knows our intentions; they judge us by our actions, and they may provide real, solid feedback. These types of questions might seem soft and unnatural (to some), especially if you are asking for feedback from those lower than you on the organization chart, but think about how you would feel when you were in their shoes if someone asked you these questions in such a way that you could tell they were serious about improving their attitude.

Enemies Are Counterproductive

What about the one person who works at your company whom you despise? You have never seen eye-to-eye with that person. They do not respect you, and you do not respect them, or that is how you see it. There may be a deep-rooted history, or there may have just been a few bad encounters. Hopefully, you do not have too many relationships like this (or at least you don't have relationships that are this severe), but there is probably at least one relationship with some potential for improvement.

Why might there be some benefit in challenging the current state of your relationship with that person?

First off, that relationship is probably causing you some level of stress. So the elimination of a source of stress is a one potential benefit. If it is someone you work with all the time, such as a direct report or a boss, it is probably providing you LOTS OF STRESS.

Second, even if you only work with that person sparingly, the current relationship status is most likely counterproductive for both of you. In fact, it might be counterproductive for everyone involved. If you see it as a bad relationship, it's probably evident to others around you.

> I destroy my enemy when I make him my friend.
>
> —*Abraham Lincoln*

Maybe old Abe is setting out a tough standard, there. Do you have to be friends with everyone at work? Probably not. That is impossible. But destroying an enemy relationship, or coming to an understanding with an enemy, can be a very rewarding experience. In some cases it can actually, as crazy as this may seem, start a friendship, as old Abe was (kind of) saying.

Sometimes we don't like to admit it, but the reason we perceive a specific person as an enemy is because that person shares one or more traits with us. It could be stubbornness or competitiveness. It could be a number of other things. The very reasons you were at odds with someone for a long time are the very reasons that there might be some real potential in that relationship.

Lastly, think about what kind of a message the act of making your enemy your friend, or at least a nonenemy, sends to others in your organization. If it were easy, everyone would be doing it. If you set out to make that relationship better YOU are CHOOSING to do it, to lead it.

How do we do this? It sounds kind of nice in theory, but in practice, even if we actually want to do it, how does one get started?

- *You have to want a better relationship.* You have to REALLY want it, because it is going to take a lot of work from you.
- *Realize that everything you have tried to date has not worked.* Let's mention the traditional definition of insanity: Doing the same thing over and over again and expecting different results. So, maybe you have TRIED some things in the past, and that is great, but you need to consider new ideas. Maybe you have not tried anything, so any idea will be new.
- *Realize that your attitude to date has not worked.* There is a reason, maybe many reasons, why you do not get along with this person. You have probably developed a negative attitude toward him or her, and you can probably come up with some valid excuses for that. The question now is: Is that attitude, the one you held when the problems and struggles were ongoing, going to be the same attitude that allows you to overcome those problems and struggles? Also, try to make sure you are not justifying your attitude toward that person just because others might agree with your feelings. That is fine, but again, will that attitude help you rectify the situation?

- *Check your ego at the door.* Why is your relationship a struggle with this person? There are probably some very good reasons, but realize that the other person probably feels the same way. The most difficult thing to be done here is to let go of the past. Let go of who is right and who is wrong. If you cannot do that, it's going to be very difficult.
- *Open up and bring some humility.* This is where you have to swallow your ego. What matters more here, your pride or bettering the situation? Maybe the best way to tackle the situation is to ask the other person how the situation should be tackled. That can be tough. Another way to get started would be to admit some shortcomings you have had in the relationship and mention those actions. That can be REALLY tough. You probably feel this person is the cause of all the problems, and maybe you are right—maybe. How far will you get if you approach the person with all the problems you have with his or her actions? Probably not very far. If you open up the door, just a little bit, with some humility by discussing some things you can do better, by asking the person for some advice, you might be truly surprised.
- *Be open to the other person's point of view and ideas.* Be creative and open to listening. Think about the situation from the other person's point of view, consider these points, and try something new. But also, you must be open to listening, and one of the real keys to making a rapprochement work is allowing the former enemy to be part of all of it: identification of the issues, brainstorming on ideas, and implementation. Those things sound real formal, huh? Basically, just work as a team. Work as a team with your enemy to improve the relationship with that enemy!
- *YOU take the first step.* Cheerleaders unite the fans and the players as ONE TEAM. Enemies on your own team are toxic to the team's potential. Enemies in your organization are toxic to the organization's potential. **If you want to be the Audit CheerLEADER, then you have to be willing to LEAD the change.**

Leadership Summary

Create a home-field advantage for your colleagues and teams:

- Demand belief! Attract belief. Decide and commit to the people in whom you want to believe, and push them to new heights.
- Welcome conflict, lead conflict, and present it as healthy and as a growth opportunity for all involved.
- Be intentional about the positivity you are exuding to your colleagues.
- Eliminate enemies through positive means.

PART II

Networking Skills

CHAPTER 5

Your Social Capital

Take out a piece of blank paper, a pen, and a pencil with an eraser. Draw a diagram like the one depicted in Figure 5.1 on your piece of paper.

If you would like, make a copy of this diagram and write directly on it.

Now, at the top of the page write the word SOCIAL CAPITAL. Right above the circle, or inside it, write the words CIRCLE OF TRUST.

What we are going to do now is map out **your** social capital. We'll get back to your drawing, but first we need you to think of yourself as an asset, which of course you are!

There are two ways we can break out the value that you have accumulated over the years based on your experiences, learning, and interactions with others: INTELLECTUAL CAPITAL and SOCIAL CAPITAL.

Whether you know it or not, you have lots of value inside you in both of these areas. Let's focus on the social side. Most auditors do not reflect on this type of capital until they need something from somebody. It's too

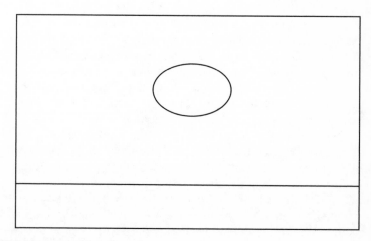

FIGURE 5.1 Social Capital Diagram

late then, kind of like wanting to buy flood insurance when you see water seeping into your basement. Let's be proactive and map out your social capital now.

Social Capital

Dictionary.com defines *social capital* as "an economic idea that refers to the connections between individuals and entities that can be economically valuable. Social networks that include people who trust and assist each other can be a powerful asset. These relationships between individuals and firms can lead to a state in which each will think of the other when something needs to be done."

This is basically your network of friends and "friendly" professional colleagues. These people may have the ability (and the **DESIRE**) to help you in your career personally, plus they have other friends who can help you as well. This help may come in the form of an introduction to someone else, an idea that could help you, or simply encouragement. They are also people you have helped, known, or worked with in one form or another in the past.

If you want to list people who would be part of your social capital, they would go above the line in the picture, but not necessarily in your circle of trust, which we'll discuss soon.

Your social capital inventory is based on people with whom you have developed a relationship. Once you have identified people who fall under this broad category, tag them somehow. If you use Outlook, consider creating a specific category called "Social Capital" or something like that. That way you will be able to filter your contacts by that category.

Consider making it one of your weekly or monthly goals to reach out to people who are on this list with whom you may not have talked in a while. Catch up to see how they are doing, what they have been up to lately, and maybe most important, whether there is anything you can do to help them in any way. If you just break out and ask them that question, it might come across as superfluous or self-serving. Listen to them, hear them, and then if there is an opportunity to help them, mention an idea.

You might be asking yourself, "Well, these are my contacts, my social capital . . . shouldn't they be helping me?" They will, or people they know will when you need them, if you have developed a two-way relationship and they know you would do the same for them.

Your list will not include everyone you have ever met. If you are unsure about whether a person fits the model, ask yourself one thing: "If I called this person and told them I had an important personal issue and wanted to get some of their time, what would their reaction be?" If you feel they would either be weirded out or not call you back, they are not going to be above your line.

Born to Be Skeptical

This whole social capital concept seems kind of forced. Why should I label people this way? Isn't that being devious?

The exercise of inventorying your social capital is meant to allow you to formally consider and document your professional relationships so that you can think about them more and discover ways to help strengthen the relationships by helping THEM. By doing that, you increase the value of your social capital.

Maybe you have heard the phrase "it's not what you know, it's who you know." It goes further than that, though. Maybe it's who you have strong relationships with that really matters. If you believe in yourself and your ability to add value to others, even professionals who are not in your industry, then you can do that and by doing it, you'll strengthen your own capital. Mapping your social capital will help you inventory the people you know and the strength of your relationships with those people. It will also allow you to reflect on the professional relationships you would like to enhance.

Your inventory of social capital might be small at first, and it might be easy for you to remember in detail all the people in it. However, as it grows, that will become more difficult. If you have someone on your list and you cannot remember anything about them, they probably should not be there. One way to help your memory is the use of pictures. A visual aid can do wonders to jog your memory. Contact tools such as Outlook have the ability to attach a picture of a person in the program. Pictures of people are found much more easily these days. Many company's Web sites are starting to include a picture of the person next to their bio. Simply copy/paste that into Outlook or whatever your contact manager is and now you have a visual reminder of that person. If you synchronize your cell phone or other PDA, the picture goes along with it. It's really neat to see a picture of a person pop up when they are giving you a call!

Web sites such as www.linkedin.com and www.plaxo.com can be great tools for keeping track of such relationships. If you don't use one already, consider checking them out.

Do you remember when we gave you the definition of social capital? There was one word that really stands out in the second sentence? Can you guess it? Go back and look. This word might be one of the most important words in your career.

The word is TRUST.

Your Circle of Trust

Your circle of trust should, by nature, be very small. These are people you know very well and in whom you can confide when needed. These are the people you can discuss your innermost feelings and secrets without fear of outside disclosure or negative consequences. They are part of your social capital, sure, but they go way beyond that. These are the people you would go to in a time of need or a time of great opportunity, when you had a major career decision to make or you were facing a crisis in your life. YOU KNOW WHO THESE PEOPLE ARE. YOUR LIST WILL PROBABLY BE SHORT. Write the names of these people in your circle. If there is nobody to write down, that is fine. For now. Reflect on your desire to have a person or people, or more people, in your circle. What would be the value in having such relationships? How could having such relationships help you? How could it help them? What can you bring to that kind of close personal relationship?

Stephen M. R. Covey, in his book *The Speed of Trust*, defines trust as a function of both character and competence. Generally speaking, if you perceive that someone has bad intentions, you might struggle in trusting them, and if you perceive that they are totally incompetent, you might struggle in trusting them as well. Character and competence are two parts of trust, although most people do not think about them that way. We tend to think of those we trust as being honest and having good intentions in our relationship with them. Covey reminds us that dependability is important, also. Does every person in your circle of trust have to have the highest character, the best intentions, and be extremely competent? Probably not, but if you have serious doubts about any of those areas, then the person probably should not be labeled in your circle. Or maybe, better yet, you should be thinking: How can they get in my circle? Maybe part of the trust is on you too. What is holding you back from trusting them? What will it take for you to trust them to the fullest? In answering those questions, you are probably on a solid path to enhancing an already good relationship.

Ask yourself another question related to your closest relationships and the circle of trust concept.

Which people would label you as part of their circle of trust?

In reflecting about that, about who would label you as such . . . what kind of a sense of fulfillment does that provide you? If someone is in your circle, does it necessarily mean you are in their circle, and vice versa? Is that okay? Is there anyone you are close to about whose level of trust you are not completely sure? Great; now, if you choose, you have an opportunity ahead of you. Uncover any barriers to a very trusting relationship, and then decide if you would like to break them down and go for it.

Strengthen Your Capital

So, how do we use this picture, these categorized people? How do we use our social capital?

One way this exercise may help is to simply give you some confidence. Listing these people will probably help you realize how fortunate you are to have as many professional friends as you already have.

Another thing you can do? YOU BUILD IT UP. You make your social capital strong, or even stronger than it currently is. What is the best way to make your capital stronger? Help make the people listed stronger. How do you do that? You ask them. What?

- How is your job doing? Your career? Is there anything I can do to help?
- Talk to me about your recent accomplishments. (Then you can ask yourself internally how much you were a part of those accomplishments. If you were a big part . . . how does that continue? If you were a small part or no part at all, how does that change?)

Look at your diagram, the names of the people you have placed inside your social capital group. Is there anyone whom you would like to be in your diagram, but isn't?

Now we'll draw a line toward the bottom of the page. Below this line you can add names of people who are not in your circle of trust, not even part of your social capital—but maybe you would like them to be! Maybe it is someone you have heard good things about, but have never had the chance to meet. Maybe it is someone who works in your industry in a position similar to yours, but at a different organization? Maybe it is a person whom a friend of yours has wanted to introduce to you, but that introduction hasn't happened yet. Maybe it is someone you met very briefly once and enjoyed talking to, but did not get enough time to get to know more.

Your social capital, if you allow it, can go far beyond the colleagues in your industry. This is where it can get fun if you want it to. Think about all the business relationships you have had over the last year or so. Have you hired a towing company to tow your car to a service station when it broke down? Have you worked with a real estate agent? Have you bought a home or refinanced a mortgage? In all of these transactions, there were individuals involved.

Do these vendors provide great customer service, and do you believe in the quality of their service? For those who do meet your high standards, identify them as such. Now, how can they be part of your social capital, and why would you want them to be part of it?

Once you have worked with them and have experienced great service, would you feel comfortable in referring their services to others? Think about it. You know of great vendors, and you have friends and others in your social capital group who will probably need those types of vendors in the future. You have previously used a vendor based on a recommendation of another, and you probably felt more comfortable in using that vendor versus someone you found on the Internet or in a phonebook. Others feel that way, too. Most likely, you already have a list of your "preferred" vendors that you keep in your contacts. Now all you have to do is categorize them as your social capital, and be aware of that when you are talking to others who might be able to benefit from using their services. What has happened? You have expanded your social capital, and now you have resources who can help others. You are building up both the vendor you referred, by helping them to get new business, but also the person to whom you were giving the referral, because you are recommending service, and since you are confident they will experience the same high-quality service, they will! All of a sudden your social capital, your social network, is expanding and strengthening.

Once you have strong social capital like that, when you need something, when you need some help, it will be there for you. Heck, you might not even have to go very far to find help. It might even come to you, especially if those people in your network are proactive like you in trying to strengthen their capital.

Leadership Summary

Use your social capital to take your leadership skills to the next level:

- Inventory your current capital, including those in your circle of trust.
- Focus on strengthening your social capital by strengthening the individuals in it.

CHAPTER 6

The First Step in Networking

The act of *networking* is defined by dictionary.com as "To cultivate people who can be helpful to one professionally, esp. in finding employment or moving to a higher position." That approach is overrated.

The best (and first) way you can create a network is to cultivate the relationships you have right now. You probably work for an accounting firm, an internal audit, a professional services firm, government, or a not-for-profit. No matter the size, I bet you are surrounded with some pretty smart, highly capable people. Some will go on to become very successful at your current employer; some of them will go on to become very successful for other employers. These are the people with whom you have the best opportunity to network, because these are the people with whom you are currently spending lots of time.

Treat every relationship with a colleague whom you work with extensively like a potential 20-year relationship.

That sounds a little—no, make it A LOT—crazy.

We don't have that many people in our ENTIRE lives where we have even 10-year relationships. Those kinds of relationships are reserved only for:

- Good friends
- People we REALLY care about
- People we want to help, inside and outside the office walls
- People we want to help succeed

People do business with friends. They do business with people who care about them, and they definitely do business with people who want to see them personally succeed. Don't you want to work with these kinds of people we are describing?

In many ways, the "20-year relationship" is not built around a relationship only at a specific company.

ASK YOURSELF RIGHT NOW: If one of the people you work with were to leave your company, would you still stay in touch? Would they want to? If the answer is always no, you might miss out on an opportunity to create a relationship that transcends jobs.

If that is the first step in building up your network, build from the inside first. Challenge your current professional relationships. Which ones can be improved? Not everyone is going to be your best friend, and not everyone is going to be a 20-year relationship, but trying to make that happen, being on the lookout for it, will help you to break down barriers of distrust that are apparent in so many organizations.

We can expand this point past professional colleagues as well. You have current relationships with friends, clients, past classmates, family, neighbors, and more. The point here is that the possibilities are numerous. The first step in networking is to network with the people you already know.

Networking Events

What if ... you are going to attend networking events? **Challenge your mind-set.**

Why do most people attend networking events? It's to expand their network.

Most of us feel we do that by finding people who can help us.

The problem is that if everyone has that attitude, nobody is going to get anywhere, because all you have is people running around trying to look out for themselves.

Instead, try and do two simple things:

1. Look for people and situations where you can put people at ease.
2. Look for people and situations where you can be **OF HELP**. (Remember that this probably isn't as hard as you think, because remember what most people want in attending networking events!)

This change in mind-set may actually make you less nervous. Many times, when people attend events, they put expectations on themselves to try and get something, whether it be new business, new contacts, or something else for themselves. Put new expectations on yourself! Expect yourself to find people that you can help!

Another thing you need to consider when attending networking events: What do you do? You know you will get that question a lot. The most common answer is: I work for so-and-so. BORING. Create your business introduction. Some people call this your elevator introduction or your laser introduction. Your laser introduction is something that will, in 15 seconds or less, tell somebody what it is you do, but it's okay if there is some CREATIVITY involved. Turn to Chapter 2, "Selling Number One," for tips on creating your laser introduction. Remember, your introduction, what you say, and especially how you say it (including your body language) combine to make that first impression.

If you can answer "What do you do?" in a pretty comfortable way, take it a step further and try and answer another similar-sounding question: "What are you doing?" or "What have you been up to?" Typically auditors will answer that type of question with a pretty simple answer, such as "I am working on the audit of ABC company." Are you trying to convey enthusiasm? What are you enjoying about the current project or audit you are performing? If the answer is nothing, then what has the project taught you? What are some of the challenges you and your team have overcome? Instead of a simple answer, you are telling a story. Think about it. The more interesting you can be, the more interested the audience will be.

Here is an example:

> *Recently, I have been working on the audit of the ___ Foundation, and there has been a lot to learn. Despite my experience in auditing not-for-profit organizations, I have never audited a foundation, and it was enjoyable to learn how they are set up and the rules that govern how dollars can be used to help the foundation to meet its mission. I have a great staff that helped me get up to speed quickly.*

While this might not be the best example ever, what does it convey to the listener? They get a taste of your (1) enthusiasm, (2) your belief in your staff, team, and organization, and (3) some of your experience.

Approach Networking as Relationship-Building

Here is another take on the term *networking*. When you hear that term, do you think about it in a positive context? Probably not. Most people don't, especially younger auditors I have met. When I was a young, green auditor, I thought networking was about going to networking events and handing my business card out to people. Seriously.

Think about networking as relationship-building. Sometimes you might be starting from ground zero, and that may be the hardest situation. You are at some event, and you know absolutely nobody. Maybe you think of it during that scenario as relationship prospecting. No, we're not talking about looking for a date; we are talking about looking for people who are interesting. Notice we did not say look for people who will find you interesting.

You might feel pressure to attend certain state CPA society meetings or attend certain industry conferences to expand your network. Sure, you want to help your organization however you can, but the best way to expand your "network" through attending events, if that is one of your goals, is to do it in a way that you feel comfortable. Some of us are introverted, some of us are extroverted, and a whole bunch of us are in between. While it is great to practice and challenge yourself to feel comfortable in networking at events like this, remember your strengths and play to them.

An event does not have to have the term *networking event* in its title for you to network. Sports events, charity functions, and organizational meetings can suffice. Many accounting firms and corporations are supporting their professionals more and more in these types of endeavors because they allow them to contribute to worthwhile causes while at the same time get their name and people out there for others to see. Choose the types of events in which you are most comfortable attending and socializing with others. You will be at ease, and people will see you in your best light.

Networking Tips for Networking Events

Prepare ahead of time to talk current events.

Prepare ahead of time to provide your business introduction and your "what you have been up to recently" answer. Maybe they are the same.

Spend quality time with people, rather than using the greet, meet, and ditch technique.

Spending quality time means attentive focus on the person with whom you are talking, not roaming eyes.

Ask people open-ended questions. Get them talking about ... them.

Repeat the person's name as much as you can. (That helps you to remember it, and it helps them to remember you. People like to hear their names.)

Get a business card, and don't be afraid to write on it (in front of them). Record notes based on what you learn about them. If you have uncovered a way to help them, make sure it is recorded and that they should expect to hear from you.

End with the same (or more) enthusiasm than you brought to the encounter when you first greeted.

Leadership Summary

- Network first by acknowledging and strengthening your current relationships ... the ones you have right now!
- Network by looking to help others instead of yourself.
- Network with others based on your strengths.

PART III

Time Management and Personal Productivity Skills

CHAPTER 7

The Most Important Word to an Auditor

What is the most important word to an auditor?

Might it be "no"? Do we say that word enough and feel comfortable about it? That concept is discussed more in Chapter 9.

Might it be "trust"? Do we analyze our trust levels with our fellow colleagues and clients enough to ensure our professional relationships are working at their maximum effectiveness? That concept is discussed more in Chapter 5.

The most important word to an auditor is ... WHY.

Many auditors excel in "doing." Do this. Do that. How do we do it? Then we want to know how. But before we answer the *how*, we must answer the *why*.

Don't be afraid to ask why!

Understand More by Asking "Why?"

If we went around the auditing world right now and asked every single auditor why were they performing an audit for the client or entity they were currently serving, what would the responses be? Some might not have a response. They have never thought about it. Sometimes, only the most senior executives involved with the audit know the answer. Sad. Why was an audit required? Who was requiring it? We don't know. We never asked why.

If you get into the habit of asking *why* more, frequently you will get in the habit of challenging tasks, concepts, and priorities. There have actually been financial statement audit planning sessions I have witnessed where that *why* question was asked, and it actually led to considering making the audit into a review or some other limited type of assurance engagement instead.

Many times auditors don't want to ask why. They are too busy. They have too much to do, so they just want to know WHAT they have to do and HOW it needs to get done. They do not want to think about the reason for doing it. We might try and justify this by saying, "It's not my job to know or ask why." But asking why and recommending better solutions establishes yourself as a leader, no matter your level.

All highly competent people continually search for ways to keep learning, growing, and improving. They do that by asking *why*. After all, the person who knows *how* will always have a job, but the person who knows *why* will always be the boss.

—*Benjamin Franklin*

Why do we perform this audit?
Why does this entity need an audit?
Why were we hired? Why were we engaged? Why does management want an audit? Why is an audit required?
Why is this an audit? Could it be agreed-upon procedures, a review, or just a compilation?
Why did we do this work paper last year?
Why do we have to wait on the client before we get started?
Why are we retaining a copy of this source record in our work papers?
Why are we testing 25 items?
Why are we performing more procedures in this area versus that other one?
Why are we just following last year's audit plan?
Why did we go over budget in this area?
Why are we using this date as a cutoff for this testing?
Why are we performing this procedure?
Why are we specifically recalculating inventory extensions here?

Why Are We Specifically Recalculating Inventory Extensions Here?

Recalculating inventory extensions ensures that the quantity multiplied by the value (usually cost) equals the extended value (again usually extended cost). Huh?! What does that have to do with anything? This simple example illustrates our need to understand the reasons. Okay, so why do we do that? The answer in simple terms may be to ensure the math is correct. Quantity * Value = Extended Value. But again, why does that matter?

Why Do We Care if the Math Is Correct?

If you are auditing an inventory financial statement balance, you need to know what it consists of, and in this case, we are assuming number of items multiplied by a value, usually a cost. We may test the number of items by performing a procedure such as an inventory count. We may also test the value (or cost) by performing some kind of price test. So, if we audited those two parts and concluded that the two numbers were reasonable, yet the numbers were INCORRECTLY multiplied, our work was worthless if we then conclude that the total value is reasonable. It is not. Sure, the two parts were stated fairly, and usually auditing those parts is what takes up the most time, but if the math is wrong, nothing else matters. The total balance is incorrectly stated. To avoid this problem, we test the math by performing recalculations or getting comfortable with the controls around the application that performs the calculations, etc. That is *why*.

*I am auditing financial statements and Revenue is 1.3 million dollars.
    Why?* (Before auditing a specific account balance, take a big-
    picture view by asking a general why about the total balance.
    Sometimes we dive into the details too quickly, and we miss seeing
    the forest from the trees.)
*I am reviewing an internal control in conjunction with an audit. Why
    am I reviewing this specific internal control?*
*Why are we having this meeting? Why is this meeting on my schedule?
    Why is a (group) meeting necessary to accomplish our objectives?*

Why . . . This Meeting?

If you start to ask why questions related to meetings, you may find yourself calling for fewer of them, attending less of them, and holding more efficient and effective meetings. Is your organization notorious for inefficient meetings, possibly unnecessary meetings, and meetings that start late and end late? Challenge them with *why*.

(continued)

(continued)

Why Are We Having This Meeting?

What are the objectives of the meeting? Why isn't there an agenda for this meeting? What are the actions we hope to take during or after the meeting? Is there anything that would prevent us from creating clear actions or making decisions? What information, if any, do we need to have, and possibly review, to prepare in advance for the meeting? What decisions, actions, and so forth do we hope to have created when the meeting is over?

Why Am I Attending This Meeting?

Do I need to be included? Who needs to be involved? Are there people invited who do not need to be included? Sitting in on meetings may not always be necessary. Having more participants does not always translate into a more efficient or higher-quality meeting; many times, it has the exact opposite effect. Who needs to attend for us to meet our specific objectives?

Why Would This Meeting Go Late?

Have a clear start and end time. How can the meeting be kept on topic? What should happen when somebody is late? (How do we reinforce the importance of promptness?) Should we designate someone to take notes? How do we get everyone energized and motivated to have an efficient meeting? How do we remind ourselves of our end time throughout and ensure we are on schedule?

Have you spent any time around a little kid lately? If so, you have probably experienced the why syndrome.

You cannot go outside yet. WHY? Because you do not have your gloves. WHY do I need them? Because you'll freeze your hands. WHY? Do you remember last time you went outside without your gloves? Yes. What happened? I was cold.

So now the little kid understands that if he or she goes outside now without gloves on, his or her hands will be cold. Now the kid gets it. It could have been a shorter conversation if the parent was able to explain the reason why on the kid's terms from the beginning, but the series of questions enabled the kid to understand.

Yet as auditors, we do not ask these questions frequently enough when doing our jobs. If we went around the auditing world right now and asked staff auditors currently performing certain audit procedures (for example, simple inquires of management) WHY they were performing such specific procedures, what would the responses be? Some might have great answers; others might be just "doing what they were told to do" or "what the audit program tells us we should do." If you don't understand the reason why, you are increasing the risk of YOU performing that specific audit procedure without the fundamental knowledge that will assist you in making good decisions and using sound judgment while performing the procedures. Challenge yourself to ask a series of *whys*.

Why are you performing that specific audit procedure? Maybe because it is in response to some kind of identified risk, but maybe there is another answer, too. Like the little kid, take the why questioning down to the lowest level you need to completely understand the answer.

> *Why am I in a bad mood this morning? (Why can't I change my mood right now? What is the cause? Is it really a big deal?)*
>
> *Why did I leave work on such a high last night? (How can that be duplicated? What did I do that helped me feel that way?)*
>
> *Why am I starting my day by opening e-mail?*
>
> *Why am I choosing to start my day doing this task?*
>
> *Why did I say yes to her request so easily without thinking it through?*
>
> *Why can't I seem to get started on this project, the most important project I need to do?*
>
> *Why don't I feel good about the conversation I just had with that staff auditor?*
>
> *Why did the staff auditor really pick up the slack for ME on that job?*
>
> *Why was that staff in such a good mood today? (Did I contribute to that? What about it can be replicated?)*
>
> *Why does Suzy love her job?*
>
> *Why do I not get along well with that one client? Why do they not get along with me?*
>
> *Why did the client ask me that question? (What was he/she really trying to accomplish by asking it?)*
>
> *Why does my day seem overscheduled?*
>
> *Why do I feel like I am out of control right now?*
>
> *Why can't I delegate this?*
>
> *Why was I continually interrupted this afternoon? Why did I allow myself to be continually interrupted this afternoon? Why did (so and so) feel like it was not a big deal to continually interrupt me this afternoon?*
>
> *Why do I have these goals today? Why DON'T I have these OTHER goals today?*

Teach Why

Experienced auditors need to explain *why* more often to junior auditors and team members.

It is too easy, sometimes, to just explain the *what* ... what needs to get done. This can be especially true when you are experiencing a time famine. "I do not have time to explain why it needs to get done, just do it!"

That leads us to a great why quote:

> Why is it there is never enough time to do a job right, but there is always enough time to do it over?
>
> —*Anonymous*

Without the why, there is no empowerment, because you have not provided the other person with information on which they can use their judgment in performing the task. That may be okay in some (very limited) situations, but it can be very dangerous in others.

Whether you are on the receiving or giving end of writing review notes for a specific audit engagement, ask yourself as you read them: **How many of these review notes and review comments are related to ensuring the preparer knew the reasons why? How many could have been eliminated if the reasons why were better explained from the beginning?** You might be surprised if you keep those questions in mind when reviewing YOUR review notes.

Why were there so many review notes? Maybe because the practice of asking *why* was not taught well enough!

Some of the generational clash that occurred when Gen-Yers flooded the marketplace was centered on the question "Why?" Some scholars feel Gen Yers (sometimes referred to as Gen "Why"ers) were allowed to question more when growing up, not only to ask that question of their parents but also to get an answer, so when they joined the workplace they continued that habit. Baby Boomers and older Gen-Xers were not accustomed to that, especially coming from people who were at "lower" levels. You don't ask why, you just do what you are told because someone higher than you on the organizational chart has told you to do it. That mind-set is being challenged, and in some cases that is a positive thing. Younger professionals feel more empowered now to ask "why?" more often. It may take more one-on-one time when delegating, planning, and supervising, but is that a bad thing? Is more knowledge transfer a bad thing?

Some WEAK answers to WHY:

■ *A document or a policy tells us to do something.* For example, we perform this procedure because it is in the off-the-shelf audit program.

■ *Because it has always been done this way.* For example, we perform this audit procedure because we did it last year.

■ *Because our boss (or client) wants it done this way.* Make sure that is not an assumption. If it is, challenge it. Challenge your boss or client if you feel it is necessary ... tactfully, of course.

Some BARRIERS to asking WHY more often:

■ *It is the path of least resistance.* It is sometimes easier not to challenge the status quo, because nobody else is doing it.

■ *You're afraid of the consequences.* If you ask why, you may have to create alternative solutions, and maybe more work is involved! There is also the chance that your *why* challenge will be challenged by others.

■ *It's not accepted in your workplace.* You have asked *why* questions in the past, and your supervisor does not like to be bothered with your questions.

Remember, change is never easy, and change does not happen without challenging the status quo, so CHOOSE to LEAD by asking why.

Become a Why person:

■ *Whenever you are delegating work, ensure the other person under-stands the reasons why.* Why are they the specific person doing it? Why does it need to be completed (how does it fit into the bigger picture)?

■ *Teach those around you to ask why, too.* Be receptive to why questions. That can be tough at times. It takes patience and sometimes confidence. Also, reinforce *why* thinking. Give praise to those who challenge the status quo with *why* questions. If someone does not want to hear about your "why" questions, talk to them about the risk of not understanding and consider providing a past example of when a "why" unanswered came back to bite the team (and the person who does not want to hear it).

■ *Whenever something does not go as you had planned ... ask yourself why.* Learn to reflect on your struggles—maybe even a simple argument with someone. If you learn to ask why, you turn struggles into learning points and you grow.

Do Your Audit Teams Ever Hold Postmortem Meetings?

This is a team review of the audit or project, and may include asking questions such as:

- How did we come out versus budget? Why?
- Did we have the appropriate resources available to us?
- Did we meet the client's expectations?
- Did we meet all of our goals? Why or why not?

The benefits of a postmortem review can be manifold, and may include identifying mistakes or inefficiencies that may be corrected going forward, and improving ways to provide good customer service.

Why is the only real source of power. Without it you are powerless.
—*The Merovingian*, The Matrix Reloaded

If you ask yourself "why" before everything you do, then you can better prioritize, challenge, and execute everything that both you and others around you do. Asking and answering why questions gives EVERYTHING that you do purpose.

Leadership Summary

Ask why, understand why, preach why, teach why. Lead by asking why, and see how it permeates into improvements, breakthrough ideas and productivity gains throughout your organization.

CHAPTER 8

The Problem with To-Do Lists

A uditors are conscientious. It is wired in our DNA. We normally show up when we are supposed to, we deliver when we need to, and we respond when we're asked to. An auditor who is not conscientious does not last very long in the field.

One of the first things we are taught in auditing is to record a list of all items that we need to get done at any moment in time. It sounds like a good idea. It's better than nothing. You probably learned the importance of one in your first week as an auditor.

Why do we create To-Do lists?

- So we will not forget what we have to get done. This is probably the biggest reason. We fear forgetting to do something, so the completeness of this list is very important. If it's something we have to do, get it on there!
- So we can feel organized.
- So we can have a record of our future responsibilities. Keeping a To-Do list in your head does not work for very long.

To-Do Lists Can Create Guilt

There are a number of reasons why a To-Do list is an incomplete tool, and in many cases an ineffective organizational and planning tool.

Many auditors express frustration about using a To-Do list. Some of the common complaints include:

There are never enough hours in the day. I always have a list of things I was planning to get done, but it never works out, and my list gets longer and longer.

My To-Do list is out of control. I never feel like I can catch up with it.

To all those people with the same challenges—and I know, many auditors feel this way—you will never catch up! Who has ever conquered their To-Do list so that every item is crossed off of it? Maybe in a dream! These points are well-made, because they capture the essence of how many of us feel about To-Do lists: They create guilt!

The real problem with To-Do lists is they do not help you do anything. They really serve as a "what am I worried about forgetting" list. They certainly do not help you reduce stress or clarify what you should be doing on a day-to-day basis.

Many times, these lists serve as a scorecard of what you still have NOT completed. How inspiring is it to review your To-Do list at the end of the day? Maybe you crossed off a few things, and maybe you felt good when you did that, but there is still a list of all the things you **did not** do today. It may serve as a scorecard of how incomplete you feel.

Create Action Lists

Review your To-Do list. Does it clarify what you need to do, or is it just a list of areas, subjects, or projects? What is the difference? You cannot do a project, you can only perform the specific action items needed to get that project started, moved along, or finished.

Try something tonight or tomorrow morning: Take your To-Do list, and for the two or three most important items, simply document what the specific action item is that you will do next. The very next thing. Make it crystal clear.

There are two very powerful reasons to do this:

First, the very act of doing so may reduce stress. You cannot control what is going on two days from now, or next week, or next month, nearly as well as you can control tomorrow or, better yet, the very next action items you are committing to do. Once you have clarified exactly what you will do next, you have a plan of action. Remember, stress can come from racing your mind into the future. It comes from the ambiguity of feeling you have too much to do and being unsure whether you can get it done, because of a lack of clarity. You know you have a lot to do in a finite period of time, but you have no idea if you will have *enough* time, because you have not clarified all the things that must occur and you must do.

But you can have confidence in your ability to do the very next thing you can to get the project rolling. Project plans are great, but even in a long, complicated project, you can still only do one thing at a time. That is all you can ever do, and that is all you will ever be able to do. Once you realize that, you will also realize that for today, you should only focus on that very next thing. I have seen too many auditors spending too much time thinking about future actions. Of course you should be thinking about your future. Remember, you can only live in the present, and you can only act in the present. You can only "do" things in the present.

> Yesterday is history, tomorrow a mystery, but today is a gift, and that is why they call it the present.
>
> *—Anonymous*

Second, an action list helps you create a daily plan for success. Instead of reviewing everything you did not get done, now you can create a plan to get the most important things done and score yourself against that plan. Be real. Most things take a lot longer than we feel they should. Create a daily plan for success and this plan should not be your To-Do list. Think of your To-Do list as your menu, but your daily plan for success is what you plan to actually eat.

You might say, "That is great, but I still have to get all those things done. All this will do is postpone those things to another day!"

That is exactly it! Now the issue is not about you trying to get through a monstrous list, but to prioritize in creating your daily success plan. Now you can be real with yourself and focus on what you decide are the highest priority items.

Also, it forces you to define the ACTIONS you want to do today. Actions are much clearer and they are much more measurable. Look at the To-Do list below. How easy "to do" are they?

- Finish Jacoby project
- Start going to the gym
- Get car fixed
- Figure out our family insurance levels
- Buy Christmas presents

Notice we have **not** said to abandon your To-Do list. For some, they do serve a purpose, as we mentioned earlier, and the biggest purpose can be getting stuff out of your head during busy times. The real power in creating a specific action list is the clarity it can provide you. It does take some time to carve out the real actions, no doubt. That is part of being a knowledge worker. It's not that hard to document what you have to get done as ambiguous projects, responsibilities, or tasks. It takes a person synthesizing those items to create the specific action items that must happen next. That is what you get paid for, it is why you are given responsibilities, and it is part of the reason why you will continue to advance in your career.

Born to Be Skeptical

What do you mean, take To-Dos and break them out into actions?

Sometime the most difficult thing about beginning a project or complex task (or picking it back up again) is exactly that—getting started. If you define for yourself the specific next action item you will perform, you have specifically created a plan to get started, one you understand. And, maybe most important, you know what to do FIRST and NEXT.

Many auditors who have tried this were skeptical at first. They say they do not have time to review their list and they don't see how changing it will help. But then, in the moment of truth on that very next day when they are SUPER busy and they have lots of meetings and interruptions hitting them all at once while they are trying to get their work done, they really struggle with the switching or refocusing time it takes to transfer their attention from one thing to another. They might be busy and stressed, and that only makes it harder to go from one task to the next. It is much easier to switch between tasks when the very first thing you need to do to get started on that next project or task (which you have not been thinking about) has been written out. There is no time spent trying to figure out what it is if you have it written, and you have an easier way to get started (and switch)! Our brains work different when we plan and when we act, especially when we feel stress during the action time. It is very difficult to plan while doing, so break up these activities and see how careful planning makes you more productive when doing.

Believe it or not, you have always had to turn To-Do lists into specific actions. If you think of a To-Do as an unprocessed input (it is usually ambiguous, but it lets me know the area or the project that I want to remind myself about), then to "process" that To-Do, you will need to create action steps. It is just very difficult to do this mental work during our busy days unless we are intentional about it. That is why taking the time to plan and process those To-Do items into actions will help.

Take a look at the examples below. On the left are the To-Do items we mentioned earlier; on the right are potential action items that have been carved out from the To-Do items.

We have extracted out specific next action items from the To-Do items. What are these action items missing? There's no indication of how important or urgent each item is. The way we answer that is to put a time clock next

To-Do List versus an Action List	
To-Do	Actions
Finish Jacoby project	Call lawyers to follow up on legal letter, number is 804-555-1357
Start going to the gym	Set alarm for 6:15 A.M. tomorrow morning
Get car fixed	Call car dealership at 703-555-2468
Figure out our family insurance levels	E-mail insurance agent to set up a meeting: fred@insuranceco555.com
Buy Christmas presents	Ask Diana what she wants for Christmas

to each action item indicating when the item needs to be completed. In the next chapter, we will talk about time-blocking. Always think about your time, and when you define the action steps, identify when will they be done and how long will it take. If you are looking for an acronym to remember this, here is one:

What is the *Specific Action Item to do Next, and the Timing?*

If you want to turn ambiguous To-Do lists into definable, achievable actions, be a "*SAINT*" to yourself.

Reconcile To-Do Lists with Goals

Another problem with To-Do lists is that they are typically reactionary. By that we mean they are normally a record of what you have been told you need to do, whether that comes from yourself or from others.

Long-term goals are proactive. They are created with a sense of where you want to go and what you want to achieve.

Now you see the problem with reconciling the two. It is tough. How many times have you looked at your daily To-Do list and reflected on the number of items that help you reach your long-term goals? If you are like most people, probably not that often, and even if you did, there would be little that was linked. That may be a hard switch to turn on, telling yourself that you are going to take your To-Do list out daily, compare it to your long-term goals, and add things as you see necessary. It's tough because of the urgency of today. You are just trying to prioritize TODAY'S TIME!

Another way to think about this is to reverse the question: How do you reconcile your goals, especially your long-term goals, with your To-Do items? Typically, long-term goals involve actions that may not seem as urgent on a day-to-day basis; therefore, you will have to be intentional and disciplined about doing them. That sounds simple, but you can only DO things in the present!

Long-Term Goals

We discuss long-term goals and your goal-setting process further in Chapter 21, but there needs to be a mechanism to allow you to continue to be aware of them, review them, and decipher how you can use today to help you achieve them. So, how often do you review your long-term goals? Should it be daily, weekly, monthly? How do you know you are on track? Ask yourself if a long-term goal-related action needs to get on your To-Do list or your action list, and how that will happen.

Prioritization of To-Dos—It's Impossible!

Another big, related problem auditors face in working with To-Do items, and, even better, laid out action items, is how to prioritize them. Have you ever seen a fellow auditor with 50-plus items on their list? If you have a list like that, how do you plan your day? If you have to review such a list every morning, how long would it take just to review all of them? How would that help you with your focus and determining priorities?

Improve the prioritization of your actions and your focus by not thinking about your tasks! Prioritize your day by thinking about the most important RESULTS and OUTCOMES you are looking to obtain. Think about the end outcomes you require. These are the most important areas and projects you should be working on today and this is the way to prioritize what actions lead you to the most important results you need. You can't prioritize actions until you know what they will ultimately produce!

Leadership Summary

To-Do lists can be ambiguous, stress-amplifying tools. Lead yourself to more clarity in your days by turning To-Do lists into specific action items. Then you will have a real plan for getting started in all the tasks you have prioritized for your day. You can only do the next thing on the list, so continue to ask yourself what that specific action is and make sure your actions are tied to the most important results and outcomes you need!

CHAPTER 9

The Power of Time-Blocking

I was in New York City, about to meet with someone at a company to see if there was a possible fit between what I do and the challenges they were facing. It was 8:30 A.M., and the meeting was scheduled for 9:00 A.M. Right before I was about to leave my hotel room and walk down Times Square, the zipper to the fly of my pants broke. A little bit of panic got hold of me. I'd only brought one pair of formal pants. I did not have time to go to a store or to get someone from the hotel to help, so I created a stop-gap solution (no joke intended there) using a few safety pins from the small sewing kit hotels provide with your lotions and shampoos. It was a nice, warm, 90-degree morning in New York that day. I left the hotel 10 minutes later than I wanted. I was walking the opposite way down a one-way street toward my destination, so the taxi cabs were no good to me. I jogged a few blocks through the city and made it to the firm with a few seconds to spare. I met the receptionist, and right before the person meeting me came out, I ducked into a bathroom, washed my sweaty face in the sink, and put a paper towel to the sweat protruding from my shirt and sport coat. Of course, with some nervousness, I closed my eyes, crossed my fingers, said a short prayer, and checked out my pants in the bathroom mirror. My sewing held. Lucky me! I was okay, and I headed back to the reception area.

I made it through my meeting, a little self-consciously, but nonetheless (compared to the worst thing that could have happened), successfully.

How could I have prepared for that situation? I could have had a second set of pants in my luggage. That is an easy answer. The harder question and answer is: How do you plan for the unplanned incident, the emergency?

You know this. In the accounting world, as with most professional vo-cations and any job for that matter, the unforeseen does happen. There may be some good ways to plan for audits, meetings, and other projects based on a "what can go wrong" mentality, but we cannot plan for everything.

Schedule Buffer Time

What we can do, though very little of us do this, is plan our days with less rigidness. What is another way I could have saved myself from stress that morning in New York? I could have provided myself with a little more "buffer" time. Fifteen more minutes would have allowed me to make a call to the hotel housekeeper and still make my meeting with a more confident "fix" in place. I planned my morning around exactly the amount of time I knew it would take to get ready and walk from the hotel to the company, based on my experience of my usual morning routine in preparing to go to work. I did not plan for anything out of the ordinary to happen.

"What is buffer time?" you ask. It is extra time you put into your schedule, because you know that days never go exactly as planned, and not all meetings will take as little time as has been allotted. Life happens. Circumstances arise. How many times has someone told you, "It will only take five minutes." How long does it normally take? A lot more. Be real. Plan for reality.

How many tasks during a typical day take LESS time than you expect to complete? Do you consistently overestimate how long something will take? Do you consistently find yourself with extra time on your hands that you did not think you would have? If the answers to those questions are yes, good for you, but the rest of us sometimes struggle in overbooking ourselves.

Use Buffers—All the Time

Use a Buffer in Making Commitments on Deadlines

Let's say someone needs a memo from you and wants it by a certain date and time. You know how it is, especially when everyone is busy—the person is probably pushing you to get it done as soon as possible, politely or not.

Once you have estimated how long it will take you to complete the memo, after considering your schedules and other obligations, work out a deadline that is LATER than you feel you can get it done. So, if you feel like it can be done by 5:00 P.M. Wednesday, agree with the other party that *Thursday* by 5:00 P.M. will work.

What if the person tries to push back on that, challenging your estimate? He or she may even have support for why it should not take you that long. What do you do—give in and agree to the earlier time?

No. Present to the person what you are trying to do. Look the other person in the eye, and pause for a second. A pause can slow down life. It really can. It can also slow down the other person, so that even if that person is crazy busy, he or she will look you in the eye and listen.

Then, try something like, "That may be possible, but that seems tight; that seems like a best-case scenario." (This is how most people come up with a deadline that is unrealistic in many cases.) "Ted [use their name], **I do not want to overpromise to you.** That is not going to help out either of us. I am comfortable committing to Thursday. If I get it completed ahead of time, I'll be sure to pass it along."

Most auditors have said that when they have an eye-to-eye conversation with someone like this and they make it a little personal in how they say it—"I do not want to overpromise to you," or "I do not want you to have to come to me on Thursday afternoon looking for your memo when I am still trying to get it done. That would mess up your schedule, because you will not have the memo when you expected it"—that the reaction is typically positive. Some have even said it was a big moment in their career, because the other party saw the careful consideration being put into the agreement.

Many times, you will need that buffer . . . especially if you have historically struggled in meeting deadlines. So, by giving yourself that buffer and including it in the expectations of those around you, you have created a more realistic goal. So many auditors, in an attempt to be responsive and to be a team player, overpromise and underdeliver in meeting deadlines. What does that do? It surely does not help the team. It breaks expectations. If it happens a lot, you will be considered unreliable in your colleagues' view. Also, maybe worst of all, it may make you feel unreliable in YOUR VIEW.

So what happens if you do get it done ahead of the agreed-upon deadline time? Well, if you are like some auditors, that may be new territory for you. Some may choose, especially if they know the other person is in a crunch and wants it as soon as possible, to go ahead and provide it ahead of time. That might feel great. If you know the person wants it when they asked for it (and their schedule may be so tight that getting it to them ahead of time might actually throw them for a loop) then wait and provide it at the deadline. Either way, you have buffered the deadline enough for yourself to know you can deliver.

If you aim to be more of an underpromiser and overdeliverer, then get intentional and consistent in providing buffers in your deadlines, EVERY TIME.

Soon, you will stop thinking about "buffers" and you will be better at estimating your time in realistic terms.

Now, taking that concept to a new level, consider setting the same kind of tone with YOUR TEAMS. Push them to underpromise with you and with clients. LEAD.

Time-Block Commitments, or Say "No!"

Many accountants are good at being yes people. We readily take on new tasks, sometimes without a second thought. Do you ever find yourself wishing you had the gall to say "no" a little more often? We are assigned a new task and we put it on our To-Do lists. Many times, we agree on a deadline. What we do not do, in many cases, is quickly analyze what the task will entail, how long it will take (including some extra buffer time), and, possibly most important, when will we commit to doing it. You are a busy person. It's not like your entire calendar is free and you are at your seat's edge just looking for another thing to do.

Try something next time before you accept or agree to a new task. Try forcing yourself to put the time needed to complete it into your calendar, right then. If you are going to do it, doesn't that mean you need to commit to the time and day needed to get it done? It is not fair to you and to your company if you blindly say yes without understanding at least a lot of the commitment you are making. If you do not have the time to even analyze the commitment before making it, then don't make the commitment. If someone is assigning something to you, get some input from them on the estimated amount of time needed to complete the task. If they have no idea, it sounds like they are trying to get you to commit to something of which they have no idea what exactly it entails. Challenge them, at a minimum, to help you understand.

Ask a few questions of the other person:

- Is this the entire scope of the project/task? Is there anything we are missing? Is there anything that might come up?
- How long do you envision this taking?

This type of behavior may be overkill for small tasks, but for projects and tasks that take longer, ensure you understand the scope before you say yes. There may also be tasks being delegated to you that aren't tasks at all but, rather, responsibilities. There is a difference. A task should already be (mostly) defined, whereas a responsibility calls for you to define the specific tasks needed.

Let's say you are a manager and you are delegating a task to a staff person. How would you feel if the person said something like, "Great, I would like to help you out, but let me just check my responsibilities and my calendar to ensure I can fully commit to doing a complete job here." If the staff person is fast at doing it, if he or she can discuss with you how much of his/her time is available based on a quick review of calendar and tasks, you will probably be impressed.

Some mangers, partners, or executives might feel bothered. Let's be real. Many times, they only want a yes or no answer, and to be honest, they only want to hear "yes." But if you are ever going to challenge them on something, it needs to be done in an organized manner in which you can actually SHOW them what you have going on already. Remember, you will never get better at saying no or finding alternatives if you NEVER practice doing it.

That is one of the benefits of time-blocking. When you time-block, you force yourself to commit to what you want by actually committing your most valuable resource: your time.

Some more considerations when you need to say "no" to somebody:

- Understand what the general purpose of the task or project was. You may be able to offer alternative solutions or different ways that you can help that take less of your time or resources.
- Think about the personality style of the person with whom you are dealing. Do they prefer directness? Do they need data to understand your decision? Do they prefer to know that you are still on their team, and that your "no" answer is not a rejection of them personally?
- Make it a positive thing. Mention how saying no is a good thing, even for the other person, or how a yes would be a bad thing, because it would bring uncertainty into both of your lives. If you are saying "no," you are also saying "yes" to your current commitments.

More Points on the Art of Saying "No"

Saying "no" is not easy for some. In fact some people really struggle with it.

- *Practice. Practice. Practice.* Many people do not have much experience saying no. Just as when you learn to ride a bike, you have to do it more often to get better at it. You can always get better, and you WILL GET BETTER, but only with practice.
- *Consider your body language.* When saying no, what should your body language be conveying? Enthusiasm or sternness? It may depend on the situation or the person. If you are going to say no, say it in a way you want to, body language included.
- *Be human!* It's hard not to be, huh? But, remember if you feel bad about it, there is nothing wrong with saying that. Chances are that if you admit you feel bad, the person asking you for a favor may better understand why you had to say no. For some, the art of saying no is so foreign that they cringe at the very thought and then cringe at the very act. Tell them how you feel, but don't allow it to overtake the way you present yourself.

Planning Your Day by Using Time-Blocking

Can you time-block your entire day with planned activities?

If you are working nine hours tomorrow, and you have nine hours worth of activities on your schedule, are you in trouble?

Take a look at the calendar below, which shows a morning schedule:

Time	Task
8:00 A.M.	Finish IT controls memo, which was not done from night before
9:00 A.M.	Staff meeting
10:00 A.M.	Client call—deferred tax issue
11:00 A.M.	Review of ABC work papers
12:00 P.M.	Lunch with Sally Auditor—mentor meeting

The potential problem with this planned agenda? It is too tight! Ask yourself a few basic, somewhat amusing, questions:

- Do you use the bathroom during the day?
- Do meetings get out on time EVERY time?
- Do you spend any time talking with colleagues about nonwork-related activities?
- Will there be any transition time needed to engage on new tasks?
- Do you drink coffee in the morning?
- Do you always start work the second you get into the office?
- Do you eat lunch? Does it take the same amount of time every day?
- Will you be taking any breaks during the day?

Be truthful and realistic. If this is your schedule, you are probably setting yourself up to fall short. Even if you planned your day in a meticulous way, with every single hour time-blocked, you know you cannot possibly get all of the things done on this schedule in the time allotted. But you probably say to yourself, "That is WHAT I MUST GET DONE. I do not have a choice." Well, your choice is to be realistic. You are not going to get it all done; invariably, some things will wait until the next day, and you will not "live" the day as planned. NEVER. EVER. So if you can decide what the most important items are for that day, and time-block them first, you will be on your way to a more realistic day.

Time-blocking seems like a logical thing to do, but an auditor's job these days is made of many projects, many aspects of which take a few minutes each—and lots of those items are totally unplanned! How do you time-block for that? You don't. You can't.

Some people refer to the time needed to respond to unplanned inquiries, to fix problems that come out of nowhere, and to answer those always-urgent requests as "firefighting" time.

Is "firefighting" part of your job? Nobody wants to be continually fighting fires, and there are probably some things we can do to minimize them, but things happen. You might not know when they will happen, just as the fire department does not know when a fire will come, but you know they *will* come—and you might even know when more fires are expected. Firefighting IS part of your job. There are lots of ways you can try and minimize being more reactive than you want to be, but let's face it, there will always be unexpected events and inquiries and needs.

Remember, it is easier to fill up time than it is to create it. In the rare case where you underschedule your day, you can probably quickly think of some things to do to use that time. If you are like a lot of accountants, that underscheduled day doesn't typically happen anyway.

What may be easier than trying to plan time to fight fires is to plan for the time when you will *not* be fighting fires. How much of your day should just be your time? How much of your day should be protected, so that you can complete the things you want to get done?

This is a tough question for some people. When the subject of protecting part of your day solely for yourself comes up, here are some typical responses:

- I must or should be available at all times during the day for staff, clients, colleagues, and so on.
- I cannot close my door. At our company we have an "open door" policy.

The key here for you to realize is this time is not SOLELY for yourself. It is for you to complete tasks that you or your clients deem important, not others. It is for you to get that work done, and, in doing so, it should enable you to be more fully engaged when dealing with others.

In reflecting on your typical work days, ask yourself some questions:

- Are you a morning person or an evening person?
- Are there certain times of the day when you would be less likely to have meetings scheduled?
- In the past, what have typically been your most productive times to "get stuff done"?
- Do your days go better if you feel really productive first thing and can wipe some tasks off of your list, or do you get a high when you finish your workday with the sense that your last few hours were really productive?

These questions may help you find your "in the zone" time, the time of an average day where you are most productive, where you are most easily able to focus. Sure, it may not always be the exact same time every day, and other factors (such as sleep, mood, lack of distractions, and so on) contribute to our productivity, but many people, when they search for it, can find a normal pattern in their day where they are more productive.

Why identify your "in the zone" time? Because that may be the time of the day to target the most important tasks you have or the ones that will take the most focus. Do you have to prepare for a really important meeting? When are you going to be in the zone to do that?

Time-Block the Most Dreaded Item on Your To-Do List First!

Brian Tracy, in his book *Eat That Frog!,* uses a frog as a metaphor for the most difficult thing you have on your To-Do list, the item on which you are most likely to procrastinate. If you "eat" that item first in your day, you will get an energy boost and gain momentum for the rest of the day. Not only do you get that most dreaded item out of the way, but you will be more productive with everything you do for the rest of your day. If you don't, the opposite happens. Try it tomorrow. Remember, discipline is sometimes doing the things you might not want to do so that you can get to everything else. Then reflect on your day, and try it the next day, and then the next . . .

Remember: Define that next action item needed to get you started on your "frog." Now you have a "plan of first attack" for the beginning of your day that sets the tone for the rest of it.

Time-Block Away Distractions

The holiday season is nearing. Time to wrap some presents! You need to accumulate the supplies you will need. You go and find the scissors, which are in a drawer—and then you notice a letter that needs to be mailed. You go to put a stamp on it and see that the dishes are not done. So you do the dishes, and then you forget why you had come near the kitchen in the first place! You forgot about the presents, and maybe even the holidays! Has this type of thing ever happened to you?

Has this happened at work? Maybe you were starting on one task when an e-mail came in that provided you with a link to a Web site. You clicked through, and then you were on the Internet so you thought about something else, maybe your fantasy football team or that e-vite party invitation you needed to respond to, and then you couldn't remember what the first task was that you wanted to start!

Following such twisting paths can be laughable, but it happens. It happens a lot—maybe to some people a lot more than others. Why does it happen? Usually, it is a lack of focus on the task that is most important for you to complete next. It can be exacerbated by feelings of being overwhelmed with the number of tasks you feel that you must complete in the near future.

Here is a question to ponder: How can you make it so that everything that is truly important is done by 10:00 A.M. tomorrow?

"No way!" you say. "Not possible!"

Consider this: Have you ever had a day where you were highly productive in the morning? The rest of the day you are walking on clouds. To achieve that productive morning, you need a deadline and a target. Most of us think about big project deadlines that are weekly or monthly. However, our attention spans are shrinking. We must adhere to a disciplined approach that will allow us to be productive hour-to-hour and minute-to-minute, rather than week-to-week. How can we adapt a deadline mind-set to our daily plans?

One idea that an auditor instituted was to use a timer during certain parts of his day. He time-blocked his task. Easy enough. He estimated that a specific task would take one hour, so he scheduled that hour in his calendar. He was meticulous—so meticulous that at times he would take out his timer and set it to go off after however many minutes he had time-blocked for that task. He even used one of those old kitchen timers! The one hour is up, the timer goes off, and he was aware of the timer throughout the hour. It made him ferociously focused on the task at hand, and he found he could get much more done when using the timer. He was "on the clock" and it made him feel responsible for every second he was taking on that task.

The scientist Werner Heisenberg taught us a principle named after him, called the Heisenberg Principle, which says that the very act of measuring and observing any phenomenon actually alters that phenomenon. The act of time-blocking and measuring and timing your progress constantly, in a meticulous way if you choose, can do the same thing. It can help you be more disciplined, less distracted, and overall more productive. COOL!

Many auditors say they are poor time "estimators." They always underestimate how much time something will actually take. That may be true, but possibly not for the reason they think. In my experience, auditors are not bad at all at estimating the time required to complete a task. They are bad at estimating the time they will spend being interrupted while trying to complete the task.

Time-block away those distractions and interruptions!

Time-Block Yourself

One of the biggest challenges auditors have presented to me is the ability to have their own time to focus on the tasks they have outlined for themselves, not last-minute requests from others. There is a balancing act that auditors must perform, juggling being accessible and setting aside time to get stuff done. Sure, these two areas/roles are not mutually exclusive. They both serve a purpose in your overall team goals. Some companies and audit firms have dabbled with an "open-door" policy that encourages folks to be as accessible as possible. Some seniors and managers have told me they do not feel comfortable closing their door. That seems kind of crazy! What does that say? It says you must be accessible to others at their whim. What about your own, possibly secluded, time to get ferociously focused on tasks you need to get done? You must be able to set time aside for that, time in which distractions can be minimized.

Born to Be Skeptical

How can I protect a certain time of the day every day, a time in which I am unavailable, when I don't know what will be going on every day?

You can't. Not every single day. However, if this is EXTREMELY important to you, then you can do it on most days. It really comes down to asking yourself if YOU are important enough to have time to yourself to get through the "stuff" you need to accomplish. How much of your day are you going to protect, without allowing others to dictate it? We are not talking about reducing the time you have available for others. Okay, we are, but it's because we want that time for others to be more intentional and to be more focused for you, because you have a plan.

Hopefully, being accessible does not always mean the same thing as fighting fires. So how do you become more *proactively accessible*? Consider that most of the "fires" will come from two sources—colleagues and clients:

- Consider setting up regularly recurring check-in times with your staff, colleagues, or boss(es). Time-block them! Include those times in both of your schedules, formally if you must, by electronically sending them a regularly recurring appointment. Not sure if they will go for it? Ask them! Tell them you are challenging some of your time-management techniques and you want to present (and receive) some ideas to make your interactions more consistent.

- Sit down with your clients and ask them about expectations for responding to their needs. How can you both be more proactive in sharing issues? Solicit ideas . . . creative ideas.

Once you can lead others on a more consistent basis by creating more formally accessible times, you suddenly open up time for yourself.

Despite what might be assumed, there is a need for role models who see everyone's time as valuable enough to challenge their daily practices with THOSE OTHER people. Tell them in whatever way you need to: During our meetings, I want to be fully engaged with assisting you as much as we decide; let's create some protocols together so I can do that, and so we BOTH can be more efficient and ENGAGED with each other!

Then your time becomes your time again.

"Fully Engaged"

What does being fully engaged with others mean? It means being fully focused on the conversation and relationship. The most important skill that allows us to be fully engaged with others is maybe the most obvious one: LISTENING. Intense, deep listening requires some behaviors that are much more difficult than they "sound," because so many of us do not practice them. Most auditors listen at a "half" level. They may be engaged in a conversation with another, but they are thinking about tasks they must get done, they are glancing at e-mails coming in their inbox, or they are readily available to be interrupted by others. This type of listening is really "information mining." You are listening just enough so that if something big is said by the other person, something that YOU might have to "react" to, then you will catch it, but everything else is secondary. You feel busy so you do not have the time to be fully engaged.

This sends two signals: (1) You do see the conversation as an opportunity to move tasks and goals forward, and (2) you do not see this other person as important. I know that sounds harsh and so many people are guilty of "half listening." However, ask yourself why you are having a conversation with someone, especially a conversation that is going to be more than just a simple question, if you are only going to be "half" there?

Here is how you deepen your listening:

- Physically block yourself off for listening time. Show them by your actions that you really care about your conversation. Consider

(continued)

(*continued*)

    lowering your laptop, closing your door, or putting your phone on "do not disturb."

- Forget about yourself for a little while. Focus on the other person.
- Go further—Listen from the other person's perspective. Instead of just trying to "mine" what is important to you, ask yourself what is important to them as they talk. Express curiosity. Maybe there is some emotion in what they are saying? Maybe there is an opportunity for you to uncover some barriers in their thinking that is slowing them (and the team) down? These types of insights are only going to be uncovered if you can listen deeply to what they are saying.

Many people do not think they have time to provide their full attention, to exhibit deep listening skills. What happens when you "half" listen? You half understand. You send a message that the other person only is worth half your time. If you are going to block time with people, why not take full advantage of that time? Why not be fully engaged?

Think about the people in your life that you really like. Think about your favorite uncle or aunt. I bet one of the skills they have is they are great listeners. They do not sort through what you are saying just to see what part affects them. They block time with you and they listen to YOU.

Leadership Summary

Time-blocking—simple in concept, but more difficult in execution—helps you plan your days and weeks in detail. It provides detailed focus to your days and at the same time enables you to be realistic with your time allocations. It helps you take charge of your days in ways that serve your priorities and limit outside distractions, and it empowers you to say no more often and to fully engage yourself in conversations with colleagues and clients. Leaders "get stuff done" because they intentionally plan it that way.

CHAPTER 10

The Power of Routines

A sk yourself if you put any of the following tasks on a To-Do list before you completed them:

- Putting socks and shoes on before heading out the door
- Brushing your teeth this morning
- Checking your e-mail once you made it into the office

Chances are most, if not all, of these tasks are second nature to you. You do not have to think about them. You do not ever spend time worrying about whether you will do them or not, and you don't need to capture them or put them on some checklist to ensure they get completed. We take them for granted. Of course I brush my teeth! Well, believe it or not, not everyone brushes their teeth. You were probably taught good hygiene habits by your parents or siblings. Maybe you floss daily, too, and those types of healthy habits are somewhat measurable when you go to the dentist. For the most part, if you brushed and flossed, you didn't have your dentist drilling holes in your teeth every other visit. You formed a habit, kept at it, and the positive results were measurable.

How do we use routines or habits in other areas of our life, and how do we use them to develop our leadership skills?

Mathematician and philosopher Alfred North Whitehead said, "Civilization advances by extending the number of operations which we can perform without thinking about them."

The same can be said for you. What you deem to be important and critical in your life can be aided by the use of powerful routines that allow you to create value and results without having to think about them, because they become habits.

Routines and Habits

First, what is a routine? And what is the difference between a routine and a habit?

A routine is a task or series of tasks, chores, or duties that are done on a regular or recurring basis or at certain intervals within a day, week, month, or year.

For our purposes, let's say a routine is intentionally set up while a habit happens automatically because it is second nature. A routine must be constructed, implemented, and adhered to, and a routine turns into a habit when you don't have to think about it much.

Do you take a vacation every year during a certain month or week? It still may require some planning, but it happens regularly every year. That would probably be classified as a routine. Brushing your teeth in the morning . . . that is a habit.

Habits are so "habitual" in nature that it actually feels unusual when you do NOT do them. Have you ever forgotten to wear a sock one day and noticed it later? Maybe not, but if you did it was weird (and maybe embarrassing and funny too).

Before we begin identifying routines to implement, let's talk about why you want to implement them. The *why* is answered in *how* routines can benefit you. Routines can support you in many ways. They allow you to:

- Complete tasks you must do periodically that help you to maintain your responsibilities at work
- Work toward bigger goals in systematic ways
- Group tasks together to complete them more efficiently
- Eventually create habits, which become more automatic; those tasks get out of your head, and completing them does not have to compete with all the other requests and tasks that are pulling at you (and your brain)

Identifying Proactive, Healthy Routines

The power of rituals—precise, consciously acquired behaviors that become automatic in our lives, fueled by a deep sense of purpose. They reduce our need to rely on our limited conscious will to take action.

—*Jim Loehr,* The Power of Full Engagement

Think back to the beginning of this book, when you identified the most important roles in your life in Chapter 1. As part of that identification, you determined why those roles were important to you, so now let's talk about how you can link their importance to your actions and the use of your time. How would it feel if you could look back after each week or each month and know exactly how you added value to those roles you deem so important? How would it feel if you knew there were certain actions you could do "automatically" to add value in those roles in the coming months, so you knew you would be gaining a feeling of fulfillment in serving those roles? So if, for example, being a great spouse to your husband or wife, or being a great mentor to your team is one of the most important roles in your life . . . WHAT DO YOU DO ABOUT THAT?

One thing you can do is create and implement systematic routines that help you add value to those roles.

Think about it this way. You identified the most important roles in your life. Identifying routines can help you best fulfill those roles, whether your roles are work-related or not. If those routines can become habits, then you will not have to think about them much. You will just do them. In doing them, you will feel the fulfillment of those roles and you will know you have a plan, a plan you do not have to worry about forgetting.

Work-life balance is identified as one of the biggest challenges by most auditors. Balance . . . is that really attainable? If *balance* means complete harmony to you, or if it means an equal amount of time spent in "work" and "life" activities, and in all of your important roles, whatever you deem those to be, then you are probably setting yourself up for disappointment.

What about thinking of it like this: How can you obtain a minimum amount of fulfillment in the various roles you have identified? Fulfillment is more emotional and does not require measuring time, but measuring how you feel about a certain role. Chances are not all of your roles are work-related; maybe most of them are not work-related. How can you feel *sufficient fulfillment* in the other roles, especially during times of stress and numerous outside commitments in your work life?

You will need to reflect on your roles and determine where you are with each one versus WHERE YOU WANT TO BE. Then you can uncover a gap—a gap in fulfillment, a gap in how you feel about that role. A gap represents an *opportunity*, a chance to close the gap by intentionally creating actions that provide fulfillment.

So what are those actions?

The answer can be partly found in routines, which can represent the minimum amount of time and/or effort you want or need to put into those other roles so that YOU will feel fulfilled during such busy times. Maybe these routines are nonnegotiable to you, because they are so important.

Let's say it is your "busy season," and you are working a lot, but getting home to read to your kids before they go to sleep is a routine you turn into a habit. Or maybe it is meeting up with your friends on Friday night. Whatever it is, it happens all the time or it happens most of the time, or when it does not happen, it feels weird because it is not the norm. It provides you with fulfillment in one of your most important roles (family- or friend-related role) while you are spending lots of time in another (work-related role). You had a tough week, maybe you wished you were at home more, but you can look back and say you made story time a priority and feel the value added to that role you serve. You can look back and say you were able to spend some quality time with your friends on Friday night. Your fulfillment is sufficient, so you should feel good about it. You proactively created a healthy habit, and you kept at it even under the toughest conditions. Awesome!

Born to Be Skeptical

Routines sound monotonous. They sound repetitive, and I want to have some spontaneity in my life!

If you desire more spontaneity, you are one of the wild ones among us auditors, but that desire may actually be a reason for implementing routines. Routines allow you to do the things you need to do in a systematic way so you get them done more efficiently, without having to think much about them. That allows you more time for nonroutine activities. Since you know you are getting a lot of important things done through the use of your routines, you will discover other time where you can just "go with the flow" or do something different, something spontaneous.

This sounds simple, but before you begin identifying routines to create and implement, you need the *desire* to do so. You might identify a lot of routines that sound good, but implementing a routine takes time and discipline, so you need a compelling reason to invest in a specific one.

In examining your own roles in particular, you may have the goal of improving the way you serve that role. Most auditors have a pretty busy work schedule, and some of their other life roles may suffer, in their eyes, due to the demands of their professional career. You might have a substantial gap between where you are in serving that role and where you want to be. If your desire to improve that role is strong, if you want to act on that desire, then your discipline in implementing routines will be stronger. Sometimes this gap may inspire you because of guilt. You feel guilty not spending more time in one of your most important roles. But is guilt the best motivator? Maybe you can visualize HOW GOOD YOU WILL FEEL once the gap is filled and the guilt is gone.

So let's look at some generic roles and some routine examples:

Roles	Routines
Spouse or boyfriend/girlfriend	"Date" nights or movie nights
	Weekly walks together
	Vacations
	Nightly talks together
Parent	Reading stories nightly
	Attending church weekly
	Making breakfast together on Sundays
	Homework time together

If you sat for the CPA exam, you probably created study routines that helped you pass the test. If you have children or you know someone who does, you probably know about the importance of using routines to get everyone ready just to get in the car to go somewhere. These are two examples of routines that reward discipline (or, if you are a parent, you might feel like they are imperative just to keep your head above water!).

Reflect on your days. What are actions that you take that contribute to productive days (as measured by you)? Are there potential time management routines that you are already doing or would like to do that can become second nature and part of your system by making them into habits?

Time Management Routines

DAILY PLANNING **Does it make sense for you to create a daily planning routine?** Will you feel more organized and productive using a structured repeatable process for planning your days?

This process can include understanding and reviewing your daily responsibilities and your open tasks, creating plans, and time-blocking that specific day.

Do you already have one? Can it be tweaked? Improved?

When are you in your best planning "mood"—at the end of the day or at the beginning? Does having a plan for tomorrow give you some closure on the current day, or are you usually running out of the office as fast as you can at the end of the day? Do you typically wake up and go into work early? Have you ever planned your day *at home* before you went into work? How did that go? Was it more effective because you were more secluded? Was it less effective because you were more distracted at home than in the office?

Do you have the tools you need to do daily planning, even on the fly? Let's say you are at an audit site or at a conference, and your computer is not accessible. Do you have a PDA or phone that allows you to perform solid planning in the same way that you could if you had your computer?

A lot of people talk about the importance of having big goals and understanding the big picture of your life. That sounds good, but in today's fast-paced world, daily planning is almost a must, especially for auditors who may have big projects and tasks but also have lots of little projects and tasks that must get completed in a timely fashion. Also, if you have "big goals," remember you can only work on them today, in the present!

Your daily plan can include a review of the big picture items in your life, your big goals, your roles, mission, and values (as discussed in Chapter 1), but focus on the specific actions and time periods of that day. Hopefully, there is some crossover!

Many auditors I have worked with believe this simple routine that sounds so easy is one of the keys to having a more productive day; they just

Time Management Reflection

How often do you reflect on your time management systems and your overall uses of your time? Time management is definitely an art, not a science. How do you ensure your organizational and prioritization tools and methods are always changing, evolving, and improving?

Some considerations:

- Don't reserve time management reflection time to conferences or classes where they talk about time management. Your time management IS your life. Want to improve your life? Improve your time management intentionally by spending some time focusing on your methods.

- A few minutes every day or once a week may be all it takes. Set aside a little time and consider just one aspect of your time management (delegation skills, planning meetings, learning new useful tips for using your calendar electronically, etc.) during that time. The key is CONTINUOUS learning about ways to improve your time utilization and your organization skills. It may be easier to do it in predictable increments rather than saying, "When I finally have a free day I am going to reengineer my entire time management system." That day may never come; how can that be more effective then continual reflection?

do not always do it, especially during stressful and busy times. However, once it is a habit, you will feel more stressed and busy when you DON'T DO IT!

How do you review those tasks and projects you have delegated to others? Should that be a routine? Should that happen daily? Again ... when?

Professional and Other Leadership Routines

- *Industry expertise*. How do you keep up on the latest trends in your industry? Reading trade publications or e-mails? Attending trade conferences? Does your organization provide information on your Intranet? If it is reading, can it be done weekly or monthly routine?
- *Technical expertise*. How do you stay current on the technical guidance that helps you improve your skills and serve clients better?
- *Mentoring*. Even if your organization does not have a formal mentoring program, do you have a mentor and a mentee? Can you set up regularly recurring meetings or lunches?

Health-Related Routines

Exercise
- Exercising a certain number of times per week
- Running a specific number of 5k or 10k races per season
- Joining a friend for a walk a specific number of times (or on specific days) each week
- Doing volunteer work that is PHYSICAL once per week or once per month

Eating
- Targeting certain weekdays to bring your lunch
- Schedule your lunches and dinners for the week ahead on Sunday nights
- Combine lunchtime with other tasks (mentor meetings, meetings with clients, new staff, etc.)

These are ideas. Read them, choose the ones that make sense for you, create your own. Remember: Routines should always support some kind of goal and/or fulfillment of a role, whether they are big or small goals. Prioritize them based on the payoff.

Multi-Fulfilling

Multitasking. We have all thought about that concept. Some think it is a good thing. Others, not so much. What about the concept of performing actions that are *multi-fulfilling*? What does that mean? Multi-fulfilling is performing single actions that can provide value in more than one of your roles in life, or help you meet more than one goal at the same time.

Some examples of routines that may be multi-fulfilling:

- Exercising with your family, friends, or spouse
- Double-dating
- Doing charitable events with your friends/colleagues at work

So, if you are short on time or you just want to "double-up" your tasks, consider the potential to feel fulfillment in multiple areas when creating and implementing healthy routines.

Give Them a Name

You may have heard people say that a person's name is the most important word in the world to them. Dale Carnegie, in his book *How to Win Friends and Influence People*, called a person's name "the **sweetest** sound to that person." It is the sweetest sound because it is THEIR name. We remember our names, and we remember catchy names.

Memorable names stick.

What is the greatest name of them all? Maybe it is the greatest reindeer of all. You recall Rudolph because of the popular Christmas stories and the song he was associated with, but you probably never think about the character as just Rudolph—it's *Rudolph the Red-Nosed Reindeer*. What a name! The name itself provokes the thought of happy times and holidays.

This goes beyond just a person's (or reindeer's) name. Providing an event or initiative a catchy name helps it to become memorable also.

Here are a few brief examples:

Brad Garlinghouse, senior vice president of Yahoo! in 2006, created a memo in which he discussed significant changes that the company was about to experience. They included downsizing and firings. The *Wall Street Journal*, *New York Times*, and other newspapers picked up the story very quickly. In it, Garlinghouse wrote about the flaws of the recent strategies of the company and stated that the company had spread its resources too thinly, like too little peanut butter on a piece of bread. It is widely thought that the name of his memo and the analogy were so creative and catchy that it helped gain the attention of everyone in the company and facilitate some of the drastic changes that the company was about to experience. The name of the memo: **The Peanut Butter Manifesto.**

On January 8, 2002, a new Federal Act was signed into U.S. law. The Act aimed at improving the performance of U.S. public schools by increasing the accountability of states, school districts, and schools, and provided parents more flexibility in choosing which schools their children could attend. The name of the Act was very powerful. You probably know it: The **No Child Left Behind Act.**

If you remember when the pluses and minuses of the new Act were being debated in the House and Senate, it was evident that the *name* was a plus for the act's proponents. How could any U.S. Congressmen or Senator oppose such a law with that name? Would you really vote "no" and leave children behind? Hardly anyone did. It passed by a vote of 381 to 41 in the House of Representatives and a vote of 87 to 10 in the U.S. Senate in December 2001.

Why do advertisers present their phone numbers as words, when possible, instead of just providing the numbers? (If you want to call the auto insurance company Geico, for example, the company tells you to call 800-947-AUTO.) Because words have more meaning to us. We remember them.

The same hold true with routines. If you feel like it is important, if you want to make it important, give it a name. Give it an authentic name, something that will mean something every time you hear it.

So if you create a simple routine, name it. Maybe the one night a week you spend playing games together with your family on Saturday evenings is GAME NIGHT! (Maybe you have a better name for it.) Everyone can relate to Game Night. If it was called Family Saturday Time, it probably would not have as much meaning. Game Night makes you think about games, about playing games, about playing your favorite games with your family. If people are thinking about a routine, they are inclined to want to do it, to make it a habit.

Give the routines that mean the most to you catchy personalized meaningful names!

Group Routines Require Group Buy-In

If your new routine is one that involves others, ask those around you who are going to take part in it for their buy-in. How do you do that? Ask them how this routine could be beneficial to them. What could Game Night mean to your family, for example? Have them describe what Game Night might mean to them, how they might feel, and what are some ideas they might have already. What are people willing to commit to? What do we need to do to make this happen? When do we schedule the first occurrence?

When should this be regularly recurring? Heck, maybe you can present the objectives and let the others create the actual routine. If they create it, they will more likely own it.

One family chose to get their kids to draw a picture of what Game Night would mean, and the little kids created a picture of the family playing board games at the kitchen table, with everyone smiling. Smiling really big. Do you think those little kids are going to look forward to Game Night, a routine they not only helped to create, but to illustrate? The picture was put up on the refrigerator with the big words GAME NIGHT on it. POWERFUL.

An internal audit department did something similar when they created "word-pictures" to help document the departments' values. They uncovered the things that they felt strongly about, such as teamwork, so they described what that word meant to them and they took photographs to help them remember visually what the word meant to them. They mounted the photographs and descriptions on the wall in a frame. It was co-created by everyone, down to the very last person, because they all contributed in the writing and they were all in the pictures. Then they created a monthly routine to submit stories of others demonstrating great teamwork. They framed some of the stories next to the pictures and word-pictures. REALLY POWERFUL.

How can a routine become really cool? When a routine turns into a habit, and then evolves into a tradition, shared by more than just you. Maybe you already have certain family traditions you practice, such as spending Independence Day at the beach with your family, or driving around in the car looking at your neighbors' Christmas lights on Christmas Eve. You probably look forward to these family traditions, and they are already in your schedule (but maybe not your calendar) because you have become so accustomed to them. It is an anomaly when they do *not* happen.

Start positive "traditions" in your life and workplace.

Create Accountability Related to Your Routines

There is a big difference between an intention or a desire and a true commitment to doing something. Take a look at Chapter 12 for more discussion on that. The point here is to be careful not to bite off more than you can chew with these ideas.

I have seen some auditors, infatuated with the idea of creating healthy routines that help them reach their goals, feel organized, and add value to their roles in life, get a little crazy . . . too crazy. They create routines centered on their health, their family, work, and so on. The key word is "create." If you have created some new routine ideas by reading this chapter, that is great. The question becomes, how do you make them happen? How do you make them happen often enough and consistently enough so that they turn into habits? You don't want to go creating routines left and right that will ultimately fail in their execution.

In a *Seinfeld* episode from 1991, Jerry Seinfeld is at a rental car branch that ran out of available cars despite his reservation. His response, "Anyone can just take reservations, it is the holding of the reservation that counts."

Anyone can create a routine, but not everyone can implement and maintain routines. Hold yourself responsible for those routines you choose to implement.

According to Stephen Covey, author of *The 7 Habits of Highly Effective People*, it takes 21 to 30 days to form a habit. Covey was referring to daily habits. If some of the routines you identified are not daily but rather weekly or monthly (or maybe even annually) then it will take much longer than 30 days to form them into habits.

Two questions:

1. How do you get started?
2. How do you maintain the execution of your routines?

How Do You Get Started?

Maybe there is a routine you have identified that you wish you could get to but just do not feel like you have the time. Exercising more is a common example. You would "like" to exercise every day, or three times a week, consistently, but you just do not feel like you have the time to do that in your busy life. First, you probably do have the time; it's just that you are deciding not to make the time to exercise. It is important that you realize that. You are prioritizing other things above exercising, and you may have some very good reasons for doing so.

Challenge the time and effort that might be required to imple-ment a healthy routine like this. If you feel that exercising means driv-ing to a gym, doing some cardio exercises, and lifting some weights, when you include a warm-up and stretching and the time to get home then you are probably talking about a lot of time. Maybe that is too much to try and implement because of your perceived time famine, maybe not.

If your goal is simply to create a consistent exercise routine, then consider just doing that, and if time is your biggest barrier, then make time less of an issue. Like many other things, the toughest part may be

(continued)

(continued)

getting started. How much time do you need to create a three-times-a-week exercise routine, or even a daily exercise routine? If time is the biggest issue, then make it a very short routine to begin. Why not start with a 10-minute speed walk or some other very short but focused activity? The routine (goal) is to exercise three times per week for a minimum of 10 minutes each time. Then the time needed is not going to be a big barrier.

If that works, then you have started a routine; and if you can find the time to expand it beyond 10 minutes, go for it. If that does not work, then maybe time was not the barrier (assuming you have 10 minutes a day to spare).

These routines, especially before they become habits, must be of high priority. You may want to start a routine, but in many cases, you will be confronted with a decision: a day or an hour where you have a routine scheduled and another one-time task that you feel is urgent pops up. The one-timer may win out unless you feel compelled to perform the routine instead. You can consider trying to schedule your routines when they will be less likely to interfere with other things you have going on, but that does not prioritize them. Actually it does—it gives them the lowest priority, because your scheduling is saying other things, ANY other things, matter more. I'll look for the most open time in my schedule. You will ALWAYS have things popping up in your schedule. Another way to go is to schedule the rest of your day AROUND the routines you deem important. You are probably doing this already in some cases.

Other routines will be easy to prioritize; especially those that help you add value to the most important roles you serve in your life (that you identified). Even those, however, will be tested when you get extremely busy. Getting started with a routine is sometimes easier than one might expect. You do it once. The more difficult part is continuing the routine, maintaining the routine, ESPECIALLY during your most busy times. Be responsible for the results. Be responsible for the routines you *choose* to implement, and be excited about the habits you *choose* to form.

How do you maintain your routine? You reflect on what works best for you. Do you need to be repetitive about revisiting your routine? Does it need to go into your calendar? Does an alarm need to go off when it is time to do it? Many times, using alarms can backfire. If an alarm goes off to perform a routine and you are right in the middle of doing something, what happens? Do you need an accountability partner? Do you need a written plan of action, something you can review consistently? Should it include your roles and your mission (defined in Chapter 1) and how maintaining your routines help you to fulfill your roles and mission? Do whatever it takes, and it may take more than one try!

Leadership Summary

Routines—intentionally created, repeatable, and consistently performed actions—can be a resource for you in efficiently adding value to the most important roles in your life, increasing the efficiency with which you perform recurring tasks, and ensuring that long-term goals are receiving focus in your daily life.

Once you have turned your leadership routines into habits, you have created an automatic system in which you consistently learn and produce, but you do not have to give it much thought. It's like brushing your teeth: You just do it!

CHAPTER 11

Do You Train Your People to Interrupt You?

You are on the telephone talking to someone. Another person comes into your office and asks, "Am I interrupting you?"

Let's reflect on that scenario. It is easy to do when you are not part of it as it is happening. OF COURSE the other person is interrupting you. Can't he or she see you are on the phone?

Let's take that even further. Now, not only are you on the phone talking to someone, but you are also, at the same time, typing on your computer. You are multitasking. Another person comes in and asks the same question: "Am I interrupting you?" *Actually*, you think, *you are the second person to interrupt me. I was typing up a memo when I received the call I am on RIGHT NOW, the first interruption!*

The "Am I interrupting you?" question is actually a courtesy. Some people will not even ask that. They will just start asking you questions, oblivious to what you are doing. Sometimes they don't even acknowledge a closed door! They need you, and they caught you, so they feel productive if they can get an answer. They need the answer because, without it, they are being held up in what they are trying to accomplish—and of course, it will only take a minute!

Let's say you answer, "Yes, you are interrupting me; can you come back in an hour?" The interruption, even if short, has happened. It's too late. You had to break your focus, and now you will have to reengage your mind on what you were doing. If your attention span is short at the time, you might even forget what you were intending to do!

It is kind of laughable but we have all been there ... on both sides!

Some of the "classic" interruption tips you have probably heard before:

- Close your door.
- Put a lot of stuff on your chair so no one can sit down.

■ Avoid conversations by telling the other person or people you "have to go to the bathroom."
■ Schedule meetings with yourself in a conference room.

The problem with these suggestions is that they are too ambiguous, may border on being dishonest, or are specific but only address the symptoms of your problem. When it comes to interruptions, the problem may be YOUR actions. We will not get very far in this chapter if you feel like interruptions are totally beyond your control. If you believe you have no ability to limit interruptions then . . . you will be correct! If you feel you have some control over them and can develop skills to get better at limiting them, then read on.

Interruption Dependence?

We live in a world where multitasking is prevalent. This is especially true in the auditing world, where we measure our success in many ways by our continual availability to respond to requests or inquiries, even when we have other things planned.

How many times a day are you interrupted? How much of your standard day is taken up by interruptions? When I ask auditors this question, they will sometimes laugh and throw out a number like 10. Then they think about it some more and throw out a larger number. They never come back with a lower number if they contemplate it longer. I wonder what that tells us. What is your number?

Would you feel like you were in the *Twilight Zone* if you were not interrupted once during an afternoon? How many of the interruptions that come your way are remarkably valuable?

Do you ever feel like you have "interruption dependence"? What is that? It is a state of mind where you actually struggle WITHOUT interruptions. Maybe you are at a point where you feel interruptions help get you through the day. Have you ever felt like you weren't sure what to do next, so you actually WELCOMED a phone call or the *ping* of a new e-mail in your inbox? If this is true, then this chapter represents a huge opportunity for you to challenge your "interruption practices."

Let's start simple. What is an interruption? It is discontinuance. An interruption is anything that forces you to lose focus on the task at hand. It can come from a number of sources: computers, fire alarms, phone calls, and, of course, people. Interruptions may be inevitable, but we have a lot of power in trying to minimize them.

Most of our interruptions come from people.

The question is: Do we train people to interrupt us?

Not consciously. We do not explicitly ask for interruptions. Those interrupting us, in most cases, have good intentions too. We do, however, allow interruptions to happen, and in many cases, we REINFORCE the behaviors of those who continually interrupt us.

Are You Too Accessible?

To be interrupted, you must first be available to be interrupted. That sounds simple, and many will say they cannot help but be available, or that they want to be accessible to those who need them, because accessibility is part of their job! Being continually available is probably not part of your job description. Being accessible enough to contribute to the goals laid out for your teams and clients might be, but there is a big difference.

How accessible do you need to be? Ask this question. Don't assume. Ask your colleagues, ask your clients. When you ask them, make sure the question goes both ways. They are busy just as you are, and if they have to answer the question, they will have that in mind when they answer your question.

I have become convinced, for example, that some of the public accountants and internal auditors I have worked with sincerely feel that being available to their colleagues and clients 24/7 is an extremely important part of their role. When they get face-to-face and ask their clients that simple question, though, they are usually surprised by the answer. So now you have a baseline from which to work. Present that to your colleagues and clients, and tell them that if a situation comes up in which they need more accessibility from you, or if they need quicker response times, then they should tell you. Wow, now you are setting clear expectations. The guesswork is gone.

What does that accessibility question have to do with interruptions? Everything. Now you will not have to take every phone call, or be on e-mail 24 hours a day so they can interrupt you. If it is an emergency—no, let me say that another way—if it is a TRUE emergency, then consider a specific communication protocol for that. One accountant I know presented the idea in a very nonconfrontational way: She told clients and colleagues they could text her on their cell phone if it was an emergency, and she asked them to put the phrase "EMERG" at the beginning of the text. She promised that if she received such a text, she would respond as quickly as she possibly could. How many of those types of text messages has she received? None to date. Not one, ever.

Ask yourself: "Do the CEO and the executives of our company have people coming to them all the time interrupting them?" Probably not. Why? Maybe because people respect their time, but also because these executives respect their own time. There are CEOs and other executives who do struggle with time management, and sometimes it is because they try to be all things to all people. Whether you are a first-year employee or an executive, your time is valuable. If you don't think so, neither will other people, and they will show you by interrupting you as much as they feel they need to.

Many auditors will say that the most inefficient place to work is . . . THE OFFICE! Why is that? Is it because when you are out at an audit site, you are focused on that audit? Isn't it also that when you are out of the office, others have less accessibility to you? When you are in the office, there are many more choices and many more interruption opportunities. Interruptions and focus are inversely related.

Don't become inaccessible, become intentionally accessible. If your job is solely to support others by being accessible all of the time, then sure, you should be looking for interruptions all day long, because that is your job! However, if you feel like you have days where you cannot accomplish the very important items YOU need to get done, and interruptions were part of the cause, then you need to schedule some nonnegotiable power time during which your tasks take precedence. For those who have never done this, you will be surprised about how little time you need to schedule to feel productive and get items accomplished. If you are starting from zero, then being intentional about two hours in the morning where you simply do not allow interruptions will provide you major liberation!

Born to Be Skeptical

This sounds crazy! I am an auditor who spends a lot of my time out at client audit sites. I cannot "protect time" once I am out there. I am at the whim of everyone else. I cannot help but be interrupted during the day.

How can you challenge that?

You need to consider your daily planning here. You only have so many hours in the day. Which of those on-site hours will be interruption-free? Do you need to tell others about it? Maybe, maybe not. Consider telling them, instead, about all the hours you *will* be free to answer questions and assist. Instead of continuous access to you, they have *defined* access, and that will force them to group their questions and come prepared. Get crazy and have them schedule time slots to meet with you. Might there be other things that come up? Sure, but a majority of what you need to get accomplished TOGETHER can happen during the formal time. And yes—you will have to do this daily. Sounds like more work? It is probably more PLANNING work than you are currently doing, but ask yourself how that planning time will pay off for you.

By being less accessible to interruptions, you may actually make yourself more accessible to important matters because you will have more time to focus on your tasks at hand. That translates into more time to focus on bigger issues versus smaller interruptions. If you can eliminate 10 interruptions from your day, think about how much time you save. If one interruption equals six minutes, and I bet it represents more time than that on average, then you have just taken an hour back in your day.

One of the biggest problems with interruptions is not that they cause you to do more work. They may, but some of it is work you need to do anyway. The biggest productivity killer with interruptions is the drain they put on your energy, both physically and emotionally. Think about a morning in which you intended to get a lot of your own personal work done, and five interruptions, from five different people, basically took up all of your time. Worse yet, maybe you experienced five different interruptions from the same person! What you did, and it is important to realize this, is you made a commitment to yourself, even if not formally, to get something done. Now you have broken that commitment, but in a difficult way, because others contributed to your lack of follow-through, leaving you feeling as though you have no control over the very promises you make to yourself. You have damaged your own self-integrity, and you feel like a victim of others. This cannot be underscored enough. This situation adds stress to your life, and it can take away your confidence and self-worth. Every time you make a promise to yourself and you keep it, you add to your self-integrity bank, but every time you do not keep that promise, you subtract from your bank. The situation can perpetuate itself, and sometimes you go down a slippery slope of self-proclaimed failure.

Some of the best time-managers I know in the world of auditing are the least accessible. Again, sounds crazy, but if you measure your effectiveness by number of *times* you deal with people and other interruptions, then efficiency and quality do not matter. However, if you can be a person who takes charge of more of your day, who is inaccessible to others more often and is able to get your work done, then I guarantee that when you are accessible to people, you will be higher on your self-integrity, you will be higher on your life, and you will be able to more FULLY ENGAGE with that person or group of people. You will be able to provide them your full focus, and they will know it. Have you ever interrupted someone and been acutely aware that the person was only half listening to you? Where is the quality and efficiency in that communication? I bet you know others who are more difficult to get hold of. Because it is hard to get in touch with them, you feel compelled to be prepared when you are able to talk with them, and you also know they will be attentive to you. Some people consider their time so valuable that you must make an argument, present an agenda, or define the objective BEFORE you are able to get their time. Why do they do that? To be rude? No, it is because they value their time and want to use it in the best way possible—and they demand the same of others. Sounds good. Who do you want to be? Both of these types of people, whether they know it or not, are training everyone around them to respect them and deal with them in two totally different ways. Again, who do you want to be?

Empower People More So They Interrupt You Less

Getting interrupted is a choice. It might not feel that way. It might feel like you have no choice. You cannot control other people. Maybe you can't control people, but you certainly can influence them, and you certainly can control what type of behavior you wish to reinforce.

Many of the interruptions you receive are questions. You are being asked for your knowledge, judgment, and your thoughts on a decision to be made, or for permission to move forward. Instead of continually answering, then, EMPOWER your team. If they learn they can come to you and ask for your answer really easily, then they will continue to do that. You have reinforced that behavior. But if you challenge them to come up with an answer on their own, then you will start to empower them. LEAD and help develop people, so that they do not need to interrupt you as much.

Let's be more specific. A person on your staff calls you up to let you know he did not receive a specific schedule the client had promised. He asks you what should be done now. What he did *not* do is spend time trying to come up with an answer. He had a problem, so he went to you. He did not push himself to be creative and try some problem-solving. You oblige him if you give him an answer. You reinforce that behavior if you provide him with an answer every time. Worse yet, if you continually allow him to pass the problem directly onto your To-Do list, you reinforce the very *act* of interrupting you, so that your staff will interrupt you without any forethought. Why shouldn't they interrupt you? They have been trained—by you—that this is the correct way to work with you.

You EMPOWER them if you tell them that you feel they can come up with an idea. Throw it back to them, not because you do not want to answer the question, but because you want them to start answering these questions. Try telling them to take a little time, come up with three ideas, and present them to you, letting you know which idea they feel is the best and why. If they are way off, then you can give them some advice. Many times, they will have a better idea than you. When that happens, make a note of it—to their face! Reinforce their new process, reinforce their growth.

What happens once you start being intentional about empowering them? They will not need to come to you for answers as often, and that means fewer interruptions. When they do come to you, they will take up less of your time, because they will have actually put some thought into possible solutions. Now, instead of relaying a problem, they are searching for affirmation of a solution, a solution **they created instead of you.**

Leadership Summary

Interruptions are your choice. Are you training others to interrupt you, or intentionally empowering them so they don't need to?

Are you "too accessible" or are you intentionally accessible when you and your teams want you to be? Consult with those who need you, and based on their needs and yours, define your accessibility—and defend your time. Schedule hours for focus on work and hours when you are available for questions and consultation.

Empower others more so they interrupt you less. Learn from interruptions. Use interruptions to help others challenge themselves to grow in their responsibilities, so they do not need to interrupt you as much.

CHAPTER 12

Do You Have Commitment Issues?

Why do people pay bucks, sometimes big bucks, to personal trainers to help them with their physical fitness routines? Is it because the personal trainer can show them many new exercises? For some, that may be one of the reasons. Another reason some people hire personal trainers is because they do not feel like they can reach their goals on their own. They are making a commitment, both in a monetary investment and to that trainer, to get in shape. If they do not get up at 6:00 A.M. and make their weekly session, they feel like the money is going down the drain, and they know the personal trainer will be at the gym waiting on them to get there. The goal might be losing a few pounds, becoming stronger, or just getting in the gym more often. The goal(s) may have been the same before without the use of a personal trainer, but now the fear of letting that person down is a motivator, possibly enough motivation to get them in the gym more consistently.

Some people like to make commitments like that to others to help push them along. If you wanted to run a marathon 12 months from now, you would find someone else with a similar goal so you could push each other. You might commit to being an assistant coach on one of your kids' sports teams, and whether you think about it formally or not, you are making a commitment to your child as well. You want to read more books, so you sign up for a book club along with a friend, with the understanding you will push each other to read the books and attend the meetings consistently.

If you do not own up to these commitments and follow through, you are not only letting yourself down, but that other person as well. The commitments are pretty clear in these cases, and it's also pretty clear when you do not follow through on them, because there are now two or more people monitoring the follow-through.

Do you know somebody who is really bad at following through on commitments? That person may have "commitment issues," in your opinion, because of how he or she deals with you in holding to these commitments. But the extent of this person's commitment issues is probably unknown to you, because you are only one of many people to whom the person makes commitments. To whom do we make the most commitments? Who do we let down in every single commitment we make and subsequently break? OURSELVES!

When you think about it, *every* commitment you make is made to yourself; whether you are making the commitment to others as well does not matter. Every commitment is also a commitment to you to uphold.

Be Aware of All Commitments

Perform a commitment inventory. Make a list of all the current commitments you have made, to date, that you have not yet fulfilled. ALL OF THEM. Even the small ones. This will get difficult.

As an example, let us say there is a closet door in one of your rooms at home that is not working correctly. Remember, a commitment does not have to be verbalized. If you told your spouse you would get that closet door fixed, that's a verbalized commitment you made. That is an easy one. That needs to go on your list. However, if that closet door is just something you told *yourself* that you intend to get fixed, THAT IS A COMMITMENT, TOO. Maybe you did not say, "I commit right now to get that closet fixed on Saturday at 3 P.M." However, you did make a commitment to yourself, however clear or unclear it might have been.

Those internal commitments are the trickiest of them all. For most people, those commitments are the easiest ones to let fall through the cracks. We don't necessarily tell ourselves we are "de-committing"—we simply do not get it done. The commitment was not made to anyone else; maybe we do not even remember much about it. It is not hurting anyone else, so when things get tight with our time, or it is something we simply do not like doing, it's easy to either not remember it or simply dismiss it in our minds.

How can you make your internal commitments clearer to yourself? The key is being more formal about what a commitment is and what it is not.

Let's summarize four steps in making a commitment:

1. Define the commitment. What is it specifically?
2. Define the importance of the commitment. Why does it matter? What does following through on that commitment do for you? Conversely, what is the cost of not following through?
3. Define the SAINT: the Specific Action Item you will do Next to get started on that commitment, and the Timing. (Read more about SAINTs in Chapter 8.)
4. Time-block the SAINT.

This process seems really formal, doesn't it? Why would one go to so much trouble to inventory the small things they want to get done?

The answer lies in discerning between a true commitment and something we just "want" to do. What may happen, and this may be a good thing, is you will let go of those semi-commitments because you have a more formalized commitment process that forces you to be honest with yourself about taking commitments seriously, so that you don't take on more than you can handle.

Many people talk a big game when it comes to wanting to do certain things, such as:

- I need to read more.
- I need to get more exercise.
- I need to eat better.
- I need to meet with my mentee(s) at work more.
- I need to spend more time with my siblings or my kids or my spouse.

These kinds of things can breed more guilt. You "intend" to do something, and what you are saying to yourself is that you are not where you want to be related to certain tasks or people. Discern between a desire and a commitment. Think of desires as brainstorming. You are presenting an idea to yourself and an ambiguous goal. It is an area you may work on improving, or something you *may* choose to get done. A commitment, on the other hand, is a CHOICE and a DECISION to get something done, to achieve a goal.

If there is something you desire to get done someday, then classify it as such. A "someday list" can be pretty empowering for those who like to document those types of items. If you are someone who likes to get things out of your head, then try using a someday list to do just that. Some people may call it a wish list, a maybe list, or something similar, but the point is that it allows you to capture ideas in a specific place you can review in the future. The idea is not lost; it will be there for you. It is out of your head and if it becomes important enough someday, it will get done. Perhaps you want to read more, or you want to exercise more, but until you are ready to make the choice and decision to do something about it, it is just a wish.

The key is that you are NOT making a commitment to yourself (or anyone else) to get it done. It may become a commitment someday, but you understand the difference—once it becomes a real commitment, you are ready to commit the time and resources necessary to get it done, or at a minimum, get it started. That is why numbers 3 and 4 on our list, defining the SAINT and time-blocking it on your calendar, are so important. The hardest part of getting started, sometimes, is taking that first step, the first action that needs to occur. Forcing yourself to define and time-block the SAINT gets you on the path to following through with your commitment.

Now you can take your commitment inventory listing and ask yourself whether each item on there is truly a commitment or just a wish. If the item is a wish, if it's not a real, formal commitment you are making, move it to the other list. This can be especially empowering when looking at your To-Do list. Does it look ridiculous? Maybe that is because there are lots of "wishes" on there. They should not be there!

Consider the difference between a "someday wish" and a commitment when you are delegating a task to someone else, whether at the office or at home. Are there colleagues, friends, and so on who, when they accept a task, always get it done? They take commitments seriously, and whether formally or not, that is how they are classifying the task, as a commitment. If you are delegating something to someone who takes it as one of those "I will get to it if I have time" type of arrangements, then realize it's a someday item and you probably cannot rely on it happening. In some cases, if you feel it is necessary, work with the other person using the four steps mentioned. Ensure that the commitment is clear, that the priority of the commitment and the benefit of it getting done (as well as the cost of it not getting done) are clear, and that the person understands how to get started, explain the SAINT concept (which can be the hardest part), and finally ensure they understand the expected timing. Here are some questions to consider in becoming comfortable with their commitment, especially if the task is more complex or when working with someone who typically says yes too easily:

- How do you get started with this? What do you think should be the first step?
- What does getting this done allow you/us to do? What happens if it does not get done?
- Do you have the time to take this on, and how does it fit within your schedule?

The blunt question that does not get asked enough when delegating something is: "Are you choosing to commit to getting this task done by this [defined] date?" Notice the use of the word "choosing." That helps the person to realize a commitment is a choice they need to make, and it puts more of the onus on them. The choice is then owned by them. If you ask a question like this, consider providing positive enforcement once they take it: "Great, I know how seriously you take formal commitments, and I am very confident you will get it done."

Habitually Undercommit

The benefits of more formally inventorying your commitments:

- You will be less likely to overcommit.
- You may make fewer commitments! So instead of "kind of" committing to something in an ambiguous way, you will catch yourself and more formally say that you are not going to make the commitment.
- You will have a process of capturing your commitments more formally, which may reduce stress because you have eliminated ambiguous half-commitments that were running through your mind in the past. Now, they are not ambiguous: They are either formal commitments or they aren't. If they are wishes, you have intentionally classified them as such.
- An inventory of commitments, once completed, will turn into an inventory of achievements. Even the small ones will make you feel good. You made a commitment in a serious way, you followed through on that commitment, and the reflection on that puts you in a better place. It will have you feeling better about yourself. You will have added value to your self-integrity bank. Every time you make a decision in the future about whether take on a new commitment, you will see that as both a risk and an opportunity. The risk is a withdrawal from your self-integrity bank and the reward is a deposit.
- People will trust you more.

A very ambitious accountant working at a Fortune 500 company was working through a busy time in his job at work, and as such he was not able to spend as much time with his wife. Sounds common, right? He decided to create a "commitment journal" where he physically writes down the commitments he makes to everyone. The person who liked it the most? His wife! It wasn't solely that she was disappointed that he was spending less time with her. She worked at a Big 4 firm, and she knew that those busy times are part of our line of work. Her disappointments stemmed from the times when her husband would say certain things were going to happen, such as being home at a certain time for dinner, and they did not happen. He did not see that as a commitment per se, he saw it as target. So when he instituted the journal he had to think formally about commitments in all areas of his life before or as he was making them. It resulted in saying "no" to his wife more (and to others for that matter). Surprising to him, she saw that as a positive thing, and she saw him as more reliable. She knew once she received a commitment from him, it was not an off-the-cuff response, but a formalized commitment that had been thought about enough to know he felt confident in getting it done.

It's interesting that saying no to people more often, especially when they know how you value your act of making commitments, may both increase the sense of trust between you and those around you and increase your self-integrity bank at the same time.

Be meticulous about identifying commitments. It is nighttime, you are about to fall asleep, and your goal tomorrow morning is to get up before work and go to the gym. You set your alarm for 5:30 A.M. Is that a commitment? You need to make that call. It seems like it is, and if you hit snooze on that alarm five times (right through your planned gym time), then you have probably broken a commitment to yourself. Maybe the commitment wasn't formally made, but your self-integrity bank may take a hit.

When You Must Break a Commitment

- Do not beat yourself up too much. It happens to all of us.
- If you are breaking a commitment to someone else, be up front about it, and communicate it as fast as you know. Ask how you can help to minimize the impact.
- Reflect on how you learn from it. Why did you overcommit? What can be changed going forward? Consider asking those involved for feedback.
- If you are simply late with something (and feel you are breaking the commitment just because you are late) make sure you do not make the same mistake twice when you agree on another deadline.

This area is a HUGE opportunity for most auditors. Sometimes we feel like part of being conscientious is being able to take on more work. Saying "yes" is sometimes too easy. Saying "no" is more difficult. But when you say "yes" with no consideration of both the real commitment and your self-integrity bank, then you are actually being less conscientious, and you are hurting both yourself and the person to whom you made the commitment.

What is the ratio of auditors who habitually overcommit to those who habitually undercommit? That ratio is probably ugly.

Be reflective about what commitment means to you. Ask yourself:

- How important is *commitment* to me? What does that word mean to me? For some, it may be a word that represents a core value.

- Does breaking commitments affect my self-integrity? Even the small ones?
- How do people associate that word (commitment) and my past actions?
- Can I get some feedback on this from my family, friends, and colleagues?

Here is something to consider if you feel like you have a tendency to overcommit to people. Mention to colleagues, or family, or friends that you are reflecting on your "commitment process" and you would like to get in a habit of being more intentional about not overcommitting to people, people just like them. Ask them if they have any examples of times when you have previously overcommitted. Ask them if they have any advice on how you can get better at undercommitting (or simply not overcommiting) in the future. Ask them how they can best go about telling you that they recognize when a "yes" might mean overcommitting? What is the potential value in doing this? First, you may get some great ideas. Second, you are setting expectations in dealing specifically with them in the future. Next time they come to you with something and you are unsure about your ability to fully commit, they will understand better if and when you say "no." Third, you may be surprised at what a great conversation that may start. Chances are that the very same person you are asking for feedback has some of the very same challenges. Some may welcome that kind of conversation with open arms and really appreciate it. Many auditors struggle with a habitual yes syndrome.

Keep in mind, the feedback process is continuous. Ask your colleagues about it once you start to make changes as well.

Think back to the personal trainer example mentioned at the beginning of this chapter. A personal trainer may help a lot of people fulfill a commitment to getting in better shape, but what probably happened, in most cases, was they first made a commitment to themselves about exercising more, and they broke it. Forget everyone else for a second. If you cannot fulfill commitments to yourself, how can you do it to others, to the people you care most about in this world?

How strong are your personal commitments to yourself?

How can you more consistently underpromise and overdeliver to yourself?

If you break commitments to yourself, will you take it hard or see it as a continued opportunity to improve in this area?

How will it feel when your personal integrity bank keeps filling up with value from all the commitments you follow through on to YOURSELF? How will that help in one very important aspect: YOUR TRUST IN YOURSELF?

Born to Be Skeptical

This sounds crazy! I have little control over all the things I need to get done.

Remember, before you go about doing anything, or taking on any new responsibility, there needs to be a commitment—even if it is informal. You need to realize every commitment is a choice. It is always a choice. YOUR CHOICE. The question to you is: "Do you respect your ability to make choices, and do others around you also respect that ability?"

Leadership Summary

What does commitment mean to you, and how do you more formally make and hold commitments in growing your leadership skills?

Be stern in keeping aware of all commitments you make. Inventory them. Challenge partial commitments. Create a "someday" list if needed.

Habitually undercommit. If you cannot understand what the commitment is, and commit the necessary time and resources, why are you making a commitment? Undercommit with deadlines. It does not affect how fast you can get a project done, but it does affect others' expectations. They will learn about your commitment process, and they will learn to trust your commitments more.

Realize that ALL commitments you make are also to yourself. Make self-integrity deposits by honoring your commitments.

CHAPTER 13

Reengineer Your E-mail Practices

Ask yourself a few questions:

- Have you ever, when asked how your day went, responded with something similar to, "I was able to get my inbox down to 25 e-mails today!"?
- Have you ever caught yourself struggling with what to do with a particular e-mail, so you basically resent it to yourself? That moves it from the bottom of your inbox back to the top, so you will see it to deal with it tomorrow. If you are clever, you can forward it to yourself, delete the original, and close your e-mail before it comes back into your inbox.
- Do you ever get a sense of struggling with what to do next in your day, so you default to checking your e-mails? Maybe something good will come across that I can get done!

These may all be signs that you have potential to improve your e-mail habits.

How Much Are You E-mailing?

E-mail is a communication tool. At its worst, it enables procrastination, inaction, information overload, poor prioritization, and lower productivity. At its best, it facilitates faster communication, including faster exchanges of critical information, and higher productivity.

Auditors are pretty dependent on e-mail to help them excel in our fast-paced world. We need instant answers and instant exchanges of knowledge in some cases, and e-mail is the tool of choice most of the time. It is ubiquitous. It allows us to communicate, no matter the time and no matter where you are. The flow and transfer of information can be more continuous, because e-mail allows us to always be connected, always be in the loop, and always feel like we are contributing.

E-mail is not going away. The amount of e-mail you receive, if you are like most knowledge workers, is increasing almost every day. Sure, there may be other tools that supplement or replace e-mail in the future, in much the same way that text messaging does today, but you probably agree that you cannot do your job well without it.

The big question you have to ask yourself right now is, "Can the way I use and process e-mail be improved? Can I see opportunities to make my system not only more efficient, but more effective?"

If you are curious to know exactly how much time you spend processing your e-mails, time yourself for a few days. Chances are that may be a difficult task because of the propensity we have to use e-mail throughout the day. That may not be a bad thing, and this chapter is not presented to tell you exactly how much time you should spend processing e-mail, when you should have your inbox open, and when you should not (though of course we will touch on those topics). As with every idea in this book, it is up to you to choose which ones you wish to implement. We want you to be more effective and efficient!

Remember we discussed in Chapter 2 how the way you write and send e-mails contributes to your own personal brand? Let's go further. Ask yourself:

How many e-mails do you receive in one day?

You can get actual numbers to these questions or make an educated estimate. Now let's do some simple math with your answer. If you are like most auditors I have come to know, you receive more than 50 e-mails per day. (For some, it is a lot more.) Let's assume you spend a short four minutes, on average, for each e-mail: that includes both reading each one and responding as needed. If we calculate the time spent processing e-mails, we get to 200 minutes per day (50 × 4). That is roughly three and a half hours per day. If you again multiply that number, this time by five days per week and 46 work weeks per year, you get to 3.5 × 5 × 46, which comes to approximately *800 hours per year* spent processing e-mails. And we did not include any time in that calculation for storing e-mails and recalling them!

Now, if your answer was more than 50 e-mails per day, your time will be more than the 800 hours we calculated in our example. Calculate yours below:

$\underline{E} \times \underline{M} \times 5$ days per week × 46 workweeks per year = _____

(E = number of e-mails per day; M = number of minutes spent per e-mail)

Of course, you may have already noted that the number is probably too low—way too low, because you probably check e-mail on weekends, holidays, and in some cases while on vacation. Still, this should give you a feel for how much time e-mail takes from you.

Now, you might say you get a lot of your work done using e-mail. It is your number one communication tool. That is probably true, and it is all the more reason to be intentional about improving your process. We are not challenging the work you need to get done, only the manner in which you choose to get it done.

If you could reduce the number of e-mails you process by a simple 10 percent, we are talking about 80 hours—two full weeks—you get back in your day and life. (Or more, depending on your calculation.) Making adjustments to your e-mail practices, even if they are small adjustments, can drastically free up time. *What would you do with that time?*

Challenge E-mails without Substance

Fifty e-mails a day also translates into more than 10,000 e-mails per year. What else do we do more than 10,000 times per year? Breathe?

As discussed, 50 e-mails per day also translates into 800 hours of your time. Now the big question: Are all of those 800 hours you spend processing e-mail productive?

Ask yourself:

- Do you receive meaningless or unnecessary e-mails?
- Do you receive ambiguous e-mails?
- Do you receive e-mails that are clearly written but you have no idea what you are supposed to do with them?
- Do you receive overly long e-mails?

If the answers to the questions above are mostly yes, ask yourself another one: Did any of the e-mails described above come regularly from your clients, colleagues, family, and friends?

One more question: Are you ready to come clean and say you have created similar e-mails yourself?

We spend more time processing e-mail than we do . . .

- Using the bathroom—I bet you were potty trained!
- Speaking—I bet you took some public speaking and communication classes.
- Eating—Your mom or dad taught you how to do this right after you were born!

How much training or coaching have you received in processing e-mails? If you are like many auditors, the answer is little to none.

What's in an E-mail?

First, let's start by listing what goes into an e-mail. While there may be many small things associated with creating e-mails, the main sections include:

- To/Cc/Bcc section (recipients)
- Subject header (topic)
- Body (message)
- Signature (ending)

Where do we start? Where do you start when you compose a new e-mail? Maybe you start by just typing the body of the e-mail. Maybe you start by selecting the recipient.

Sometimes you may start with the subject header, and that is where we will start.

E-mail Subject Headers

What Is in an E-mail Subject Header?

Typically, not too much. There is so much potential for that little line. You must ask yourself a question before you create your subject header and before you start writing your e-mail: What do you want? If the answer is nothing, then challenge the necessity of the e-mail. If the answer is something, get very bold and tell them what it is right in the subject. That is right, clarify your CALL TO ACTION and tell them what it is first thing. Remember your recipient. That person you are sending this e-mail to is also looking at an inbox with 49-plus other e-mails in it. Most people process e-mails by first looking at their inbox, which is typically set up in a way that shows us the Sender, Subject, Received Date, Attachment, and so forth for each e-mail. So the first level of processing we do is by looking at the e-mails in our inbox and the subject and sender are the most noteworthy pieces of information.

Have you ever received any (non-spam) e-mails with subjects similar to any of the following?

RE: lunch

Hello

Hey there!

Catching up

RE: Our conversation

A thought

How do these subjects help you to efficiently read and process your e-mails? They probably don't. If we can create much stronger subjects, we make it easier on the readers. We will also force ourselves to get to the point much quicker. We will have to answer that simple question: What do we want right away, before we even start typing the e-mail? As we mentioned, the act of having to answer that question and provide a bold and very direct subject may in itself lessen the number of e-mails you send. Remember, just cutting out a few e-mails will translate into lots of time saved over a year.

Now let's look at some of the common e-mail practices and challenge them using the need for a call to action.

"THANK YOU" E-MAILS   How many "thank-you" e-mails have you sent or received? The e-mail itself is simple. There might not be anything to it except a reply to a long e-mail thread with the one simple word: "Thanks!" Someone is trying to show their appreciation. While it is probably the laziest way to express real appreciation, it is efficient (at least it seems to be), and who are we to challenge that positive expression? Once you reflect on it, though, you may, like many successful leaders, choose to eliminate thank-you e-mails altogether and look for other, more meaningful ways to express true appreciation.

Let's say you want to show appreciation in an e-mail. The call to action is basically for others to understand your gratitude. How can you do that most efficiently? Say "thanks" in the subject header. If that is all you are saying, consider adding something to imply that is the message, and there is no need to read further. Add a notation: "—end of message—", or "EOM" for short. Some Internet-savvy people understand that a * signifies that the subject *is* the message. That is it. I am thanking you! That is it. "Thanks! EOM." means there is no reason for me to take up any more of your time making you open the e-mail. You understand my gratitude, and now you can delete the e-mail without ever opening it.

It seems like a small thing, but if everyone cut down their thank-you (only) e-mails, we'd save hundreds of thousands of e-mails over a year. If everyone, at a minimum, moved the "thank you" to the subject line, saving the reader from opening the e-mail, we'd save lots of time as well.

OTHER COMMON E-MAILS   What are some other common e-mail practices you may challenge?

Reply to All: Is it really necessary in all cases? This is where the call to action really comes into play. If you do not know what people are supposed to do with your e-mail, do they need to receive it?

For Your Information: An FYI e-mail is only useful if it is actionable information at some point. Many auditors err on the conservative side here; unsure whether a person needs the information or might find it useful (now or in the future), they send it just in case. How many of the FYI e-mails you receive are unnecessary? Use some judgment with these.

Updates: Remember, e-mail is not always the best forum for keeping someone up to date on the status of projects or communications, and an update e-mail is different than an FYI e-mail. An update e-mail may have a specific call to action, while an FYI e-mail almost never has a call to action.

Out of Office AutoReplys: These may serve a solid purpose. There does not need to be ANY information in the body of the e-mail. Supply all the information in the subject. (Most people will not look past it anyway when they receive one of these.)

PROVIDE URGENCY HINTS IN YOUR E-MAILS   Is there anything else we can do with the subject to make it stronger?

If you have documented your call to action, how about saying or at least supplying some guidance on when you need this action to be performed. You have to be bold again. Tell them what you want and tell them WHEN you want it. You do not necessarily have to demand an exact deadline every time, although many auditors have said they prefer for people to tell them WHEN something is needed. Maybe there is a deadline deficit disorder with many of the requests that are made of us. How do we know about the urgency of the call to action without a hint about when it is needed? As with other tasks we struggle to prioritize, it will just be put at the end of our To-Do list.

Include the required turnaround time in the subject of the e-mail. If you need a task done by a particular time, tell the recipient. If you need someone to respond to an e-mail by Friday at 4:00 P.M., include that in the subject! If you are wary about demanding such a deadline and have a little bit of leeway with your request and you know the recipient has other competing priorities, then include a request in the e-mail (or the subject) to let you know if the deadline cannot be made.

How can you ask for a reply date or a deadline on every e-mail? That sounds crazy. What is crazy, though, is not supplying a deadline. Let it be up to the receiver to tell you the deadline will not work. It is still negotiable in many cases. What you have done by supplying an initial deadline date is help the person understand the urgency. Remember, many times when we talk in person and decide on next action steps, we come to agreement on when those things will be done. Why not do the same with your e-mail requests? Sometimes it is a lot harder for those who receive e-mails without any clue as to when the task needs to be accomplished. Be clear. Be crystal clear.

What is the call to action, and when does it need to happen? Try and answer that in every e-mail you send. You may find yourself spending more time in developing your subject. Maybe much more time. It will force you to be very direct and uncover the meanings behind your e-mails. There is no doubt your subjects will be longer and, at the same time, the body of your e-mail will be shorter and easier to write.

Below are some example subject headers that provide some stronger language:

- Provide feedback on this deferred revenue memo by 6-16
- Request for a copy of the evaluations from the seminar yesterday, let me know by 8-10-09
- RE: game this Sat., I'll drive, let me know by tomorrow if 10:00 A.M. is not a good time
- Lunch Friday confirmed: 11:45 A.M. at Jack's Bistro (EOM)

The above examples may not be perfect, but in each case, the reader can tell by simply and quickly looking at the subject both what the call to action is and when it is required (or requested) to be done. In most cases, especially with the last example, you do not even have to open up the e-mail to know what to do with it. Maybe that is true of the others as well. Your "processing" of these inputs can be really sped up with subject headers like this.

Think about opening your inbox tomorrow. How much easier would it be if every e-mail had a strong subject header? You know what the e-mail is about, what the sender is asking, and when they are asking for it. Wow! They are being direct. No beating around the bush. I can tell from the subject what they want from me and when they want it.

E-mail Body

What goes in an e-mail? Once you have clearly defined your call to action all you need to do now is fill in the blanks. Make them as brief as possible. One rule to consider is making your e-mails one (preview) page or less. The reader will never have to scroll down. (Many readers will not do that anyway, even if you write more than that.) Another general rule to consider is sticking to one topic per e-mail. We receive so many e-mails that you know how hard it is to keep track of e-mails with totally different topics. It also makes it easier to extract the most important thing—the action required of you—if it is one topic.

E-mail Habits of Others

Now the question is, how do you tell everyone else to do this? You can't. Even if you reached out to a lot of the people you know, there will always be new people sending you e-mails. You could send out a memo on e-mail writing procedures, or hold a small seminar on the subject with your colleagues, but that may or may not be effective, especially right away. Consider simply starting with yourself. Be diligent in some of these practices. Your colleagues will notice. Some will ask you about it. When they do ask, get feedback! Ask them if the subjects are making their life easier. Ask them what they like about them, and if there is anything that can be improved. By asking them for feedback, you are getting them to reflect on what is in a good subject line. You are not telling them what to do, and you are not telling them what they should do. If you choose to implement this idea, it will not be because it was presented in this book, it will be because YOU see the value in doing it. Not everyone will notice, and not everyone will pick up on it and reflect on their own methods. Some will think it is a waste of time. They can't talk about that. They have too many e-mails to get through! Some will notice. Some may inquire. Lead by example. If they ask why you are making changes, tell them your reason (e.g., you want to reduce e-mail processing time, you wish to be clearer in your communications, etc.). Lead positive CHANGE by example.

Take a look at the e-mail excerpt below. This is slightly modified, but is based on a real e-mail.

This e-mail was sent late on a Sunday night. How many e-mails do you have waiting for you on a typical Monday morning? This was one of many e-mails sitting in this auditor's inbox on that particular Monday morning.

From: _____ [mailto:_____.com]
Sent: Sunday, September 07, 2008 11:39 PM

To: _____

If we do not get that confirmation returned by Wednesday, we are in *&#$#$%$ trouble. Make sure you follow up with Jim tomorrow morning first thing. He needs to get on the phone and get them on it right away, or else he will not be getting his reports when he needs them.

Take a guess at the e-mail subject that accompanied this e-mail.
No joke: It was "RE: good meeting."
Last but not least, think about how much easier it will be for you to locate filed or archived e-mails if the subject actually refers to what the e-mail is about.

Some people may say, "I do not have time to worry about subject headers; I have too many e-mails to respond to and send!" Exactly. You may not have time because you are stuck in a habit of reacting and responding, instead of taking charge of the communication process. If you cannot answer the question "What do I want from this communication?" why are you continually responding? It is probably because that is what you are accustomed to, and it requires less thought. Take charge of the e-mail "conversation" by insisting that *you* define the purpose *right away*!

Processing E-mail

Let's explore ways to reengineer your e-mail processing methods so you can plow through e-mails every time you open your inbox.

Your e-mail inbox . . . how much time do you spend in a typical week in there? If you are like most auditors, you probably spend more time working your inbox than doing anything else. That is not necessarily, in and of itself, a bad thing. The question is, can you be more efficient at processing e-mails? If you feel like the answer is no, go ahead and skip the rest of this chapter, as you probably live an awesome life and are able to get more done than the rest of us in less time.

When you process your incoming e-mails, do you look at them one by one? There are a few trains of thought here. If you have lots of e-mails with strong subject headers, you can probably look through your list and open up the highest-priority items based on your review. This is probably not realistic, as many e-mails will not contain all that you need to know in the subject header.

Try going through each e-mail one by one. Think of an e-mail as an "input" in your life that needs to be processed. You want to decipher which action you need to do based on the e-mail. When you open an e-mail, there are probably five things you can do with it: Delete it, Do it, Defer it, Delegate it, or Dump it (sometimes known as the 5 Ds).

Delete It

This is usually the easiest one. I have spent time with auditors while they process e-mail, and many times that is the first thing they look for in their inbox. Which of these e-mails can be deleted? You can go through and just delete them, but for this exercise, we are going through your e-mails one by one. No cherry-picking the easy ones. Read the e-mail, and if there is no call to action for you or any reason to store it, then delete it.

What Is Your Inbox?

Try not to make your inbox also serve as your "indecision" or your "in-action" box. You have received an e-mail, and it may or may not be important, but you do not know what to do with it. What do you do? Nothing. You leave it there, which forces your brain to reprocess it every single time you reopen your inbox. Even if it just takes a few seconds for you to remember what it was, you are processing it, again and again. These e-mails are typically not even the most important in your inbox; they are just the ones for which it's unclear what needs to happen, because you want to remind yourself to think about it more, or because you want that e-mail in your inbox to serve as some kind of ambiguous To-Do item. That indecision does one more thing. It adds stress!

Take an inventory of your current inbox right now.

- How many e-mails are in there?
- How many e-mails are in there that were also in there last week? Last month? Last year?
- How many e-mails could be classified as difficult decisions not made yet?
- How many e-mails could be classified as To-Do items?

If you answered the above questions with lots of high numbers, chances are your inbox is serving multiple functions. Reflect on your desire and ability to make changes, and see your inbox as an "input" box, where you will read and process those inputs ONCE! That might feel VERY uncomfortable at first, as you are probably accustomed to touching certain e-mails many times. For many, indecision has become a habit in using e-mail. You read an e-mail and do not process it. You might think about it in your mind but you leave it there for re-processing later. Habits are hard to break.

You will need to have a system that allows you to aggregate all the important actions you will need to perform once you have FULLY processed that input. But if you can get there (and read on to learn more), then you can save yourself large amounts of time by processing your e-mails one by one in your inbox . . . ONE TIME EACH!

Do It

If an action is required of you, you are either going to do it, defer it, or delegate it. If the action takes a certain amount of time or less, such as one minute, it is probably most efficient to do it right then. DONE. The e-mail should be gone, because the most important thing has happened. You acted on that e-mail. Remember, keep it simple, and move on to the specific action item you will do next. You decide on your time limit for actions that you will do right then and there. Is it one minute, two minutes, five minutes?

Defer It!

Maybe the action will take a long time and you need to do it on another day. Maybe you are waiting on someone else before you can take action. (That is a common answer auditors tell me when they look at their systems.) Maybe you cannot complete the action now because you must be physically someplace else to do it. There are lots of reasons why an action may need to be deferred. Fine. No problem. But you must have a system to be able to defer the action, and you do not know what the next action is unless you define it. So, once again, define the specific action item you will do next. Now you need to document the e-mail so it is "in your schedule." How might you do that? Some will simply put it into their calendar. They will time-block it. That is fine, but there is an issue with doing that.

First, it is in your calendar, and if you want to review your list of action items at any day and time, you would have to look at your calendar and find them. If the goal is to reduce stress, we want you to have confidence that once something has been "captured," you do not have to worry about it again. How many times has an e-mail or something else triggered you to remember something you need to do? Okay, now you have to record that. Why wasn't it recorded in the first place? Probably because you did not clearly define the specific action item you would do next. Probably because you left an e-mail in your inbox and that served as your reminder that something needed to be done, but you did not define it, so once again you have made it harder on yourself and added ambiguity and stress to your day. You know the e-mail triggers a need to do something, but you did not have time to define it. Deferring it does not mean not defining it; it simply means making the choice to act in the future rather than now. You still must process the e-mail and define the action.

What you can consider is keeping a list of your action items to be completed. That way, you zap the e-mail by extracting the most important thing—what you will have to do! Also, you will have a list of clearly defined actions that can be reviewed when you do your daily and weekly time-blocking (see Chapter 9).

Dump It!

This is the same as filing it. (Filing does not start with a D, thus the need to call it dumping.) Some e-mails may serve as future reference. Some e-mails you want to hold onto "just in case." While it's possible that you can challenge the number of e-mails that fall into this category, there will always be a need to save some information that is not currently actionable but could be useful to have in the future. The key to having confidence in filing e-mails is having confidence in your filing system. It is easy to just file something, but more difficult to be able to call up that e-mail again very quickly in the future.

Remember one thing—with the powerful search options on computers these days, e-mails can be found pretty quickly based on key words, but who knows what the keys words are? Powerful, to-the-point subject headings may help, but not always.

This is definitely not a one-size-fits-all answer. You may have a filing system that works, and you may have many folders created in your inbox. If you can file and retrieve e-mails instantly, then continue doing what you are doing. If you are looking for different ideas, we present a few here.

Your Filing System

There are lots of different ways you can choose to organize the folders you create to file e-mails. The key is being able to efficiently recall those e-mails when they are needed. If you are filing them, you are saying there is a good chance you will need them in the future, so you need to have a system that will allow for you to know, instantaneously, where that particular e-mail will be.

Here are some tips to consider:

- **Be consistent in your filing systems.** If you have a hard-copy filing system, such as a credenza with file folders, try to have your electronic filing system mirror your hard-copy system. If you file e-mails in folders in your e-mail application, have that mirror your filing system for documents on your hard-drive.
- **File like you think.** Some people will literally have folders in alphabetical order based on a keyword. That keyword needs to be the word you will not only file e-mails under but also the one that will be triggered instantly when you need to go find it, as well. Folders can be created by name or subject, or both. Some people will have general subject folders such as "Clients" and "Admin," and

then have more detailed folders, possibly by name, underneath those. If you are good at finding e-mails quickly, then you will need fewer folders. If you are poor at that, use more folders and subfolders. It will require more time to navigate such a system, but fewer e-mails will be in the lowest-level folder, allowing you to find the particular one you want faster.

- **Challenge a propensity to "overfile."** Remember, e-mail is not a journal. If you are going to file it, there must be a potential reason you might need it in the future. Do not confuse filing e-mails with identifying To-Do items or actions. Those are part of your planning and should be captured and kept separately. Filing an e-mail will never help you "do" something. It is only a resource for later.

Delegate It!

If, after reading the e-mail, you have defined what needs to get done but someone else needs to do it, then you can delegate the work. So what does that have to do with the e-mail you are processing? For you to feel comfortable deleting the e-mail or dumping it (filing it), you will probably need a record somewhere of the delegation. After all, many auditors will keep that e-mail in their inbox to remind them of the delegation. If you do not want to plow through the same e-mails after the delegation has been made, you must have somewhere to document it. What is important?

- What is the task being delegated?
- When should you expect it to be done? (Assuming this was communicated to them)
- When did you last communicate with this person on the task?

Consider creating a delegation list or chart that would include all of the tasks that were given to someone else to complete. Once you have such a list, you can review it whenever you want to, so there is no need to keep that e-mail in your inbox. It is gone! Now, maybe you choose to keep track of these delegations another way, but make sure you do it in a way that allows you to zap the e-mail (input) that instigated the delegation and keep track of the delegation instead. That way you do not have to keep track of the information in your head, and you can review your delegations list periodically for follow-up and tracking purposes.

Delegation

How do you record and track the items you delegate to others? First, ask yourself, "What needs to be recorded when I delegate something?" Some items to consider include:

- *Who* was it delegated to?
- *What* is the item being delegated? Or sometimes, more importantly, what is the end product you need to receive from the other person?
- *When* did you both decide the task would be completed? Another thing to consider here when you delegate ... when should you be notified that the task will not be delivered when agreed to? If you are reviewing your delegation list regularly, this information may be key in following up with that person.
- *When* was the last time the task was discussed?

How Often Should You Check E-mail?

This can be a controversial question. Using e-mail is so ingrained in many of us that for someone to tell you exactly when you should check e-mails ... well, that is not always going to work. Though some people try!

Some considerations:

- *What are others' expected response times?*

    As we mentioned earlier, you need to get with your colleagues and clients and understand their general expectations about responses. That takes precedence. E-mail is a tool that allows you to respond, but e-mail should not dictate your response times. Solid client service and solid teamwork aspirations should.

- *Do you work better with your e-mail continuously open or when you close it sometimes?*

    Many people will say they get more done with their e-mail closed. Others will say they cannot close their e-mail, because it is part of Outlook, and whether it is working with tasks or their calendar or something else, they need to use Outlook for a majority of their day. Remember, checking your inbox is always a choice. You can turn off notifications. If you are going to allow for those types of interruptions, then be intentional about it.

Try something new and see how it goes: If you are a continuous checker, then try checking your e-mail four or five times, or less, per day and see how that goes. This may make you VERY uncomfortable at first. Open your e-mail and process your e-mails using the five Ds. Get through all your incoming e-mails, or set a time limit and then close your e-mail. Even if you check it five times a day and allow for half an hour each time, you still may save yourself some time compared to all the time that results from having e-mail open throughout the day and continually reading and responding *as the e-mails come in*, which you cannot control. Instead of e-mail being an interruption tool, it now becomes a proactive communication tool.

Actually, the biggest challenge many auditors face in checking their e-mail may be that they do not focus on e-mail enough when they do it. What does that mean? If you are checking e-mail "on the side" as you do other things, then first it may serve as an interruption to break your focus on those other things you are doing. But also, how efficient can you be at processing e-mails when you are not *fully focusing* on processing e-mails?

Fully focusing on processing e-mails in your inbox within a given time block also lends itself to only checking e-mail at certain times of the day. Let's compare Ted Auditor and Lisa Auditor.

Ted Auditor, E-mail Addict

Ted Auditor is a 35-year-old male. He checks e-mail on his laptop and his BlackBerry. When does he check e-mail? A better question might be, when does he *not* check e-mail? He is really not in control of the checking; e-mail checks him, by pinging him throughout the day. On his laptop, a *ping* sounds when an e-mail comes in, and the new message image shows up in the bottom right hand corner of his computer screen. His BlackBerry vibrates when a new e-mail arrives. He has his BlackBerry set to automatically send/receive every five minutes, which means it basically vibrates every five minutes throughout the day. Sometimes he remembers to turn the vibration off during meetings, but lately he does not do that much anymore and doesn't think twice about it when it happens. If it is a really important meeting he will only glance at his BlackBerry. If it is not a really important meeting (in his eyes), he will check the e-mails during the meeting after the vibration. He cherry-picks e-mails by looking first for e-mails that can be deleted or answered quickly. The other ones, the "harder" ones, he'll typically read once and leave them there so he can read them later and decide what to do with them.

He never reflects on his e-mail habits, but if you were to ask him about the subject, he would probably respond with some comments such as:

- "I am too important to ever be dark." (For those who do not know what that term means, it signifies you are offline or not accessible through e-mail or texting.) Thus, Ted is "on" e-mail all day, and also at night.
- "Most of my job is conducted via e-mail." When Ted is unsure about what to do next, he checks his e-mail, and something usually pops up.
- "My inbox is out of control just like anyone else's would be who receive 50+ e-mails a day." Ted has over 500 emails in his inbox and feels good about the work he has done to get it down to that number.
- "My colleagues and clients expect instantaneous answers from me." (This expectation is based on his past habits.) Sometimes a person will pop into Ted's office and ask, "Did you get my e-mail?" if it has been more than 10 minutes since they sent it.

Ted feels so busy, and e-mail is his number one communication tool; just keeping up with everything he has to do requires continuous connectivity and responsiveness. He cannot imagine it any other way. He responds quickly to all "easy" e-mails, though most of the time he does so by telling others when he will get back to them.

Lisa Auditor, E-mail Destroyer

Lisa Auditor is also 35 years old. She, too, conducts most of her communications via e-mail. She sees e-mail as a productivity tool that is just one of the many resources that allow her to get things done quickly and effectively.

She has reflected on her e-mail habits and if you ask her about them, she will respond:

- "My e-mail habits have evolved as I have become more experienced." Lisa tries new things and even asks for feedback, when she can, from her colleagues on her e-mail habits. Her system is by no means perfect, but she is always improving it.
- "My time and my clients' time is too important to be answering e-mails all day."
- "My inbox is under control despite the 50+ e-mails that come through every day, because I pride myself on only touching things once." Lisa sees this as a big advantage versus where she was before, as it frees up a lot of her time to do the actions she sees as high priority.
- "I routinely check e-mail three times a day: once in the morning, once at midday, and once in the late afternoon. Sometimes a little bit less when I am at a conference or out of town. It does not always happen

at the exact same time, and some days it might only be twice and other days it might be four times." Lisa will occasionally check e-mail on her iPhone when not on her laptop, but she limits that because she has not been able to move her full system over to her iPhone yet.

■ "My colleagues and clients expect me to get back to them by the next day, in most cases." This is mostly because she has talked to them about response times.

It is very easy to continue down the same road you are going with your e-mail processing system. It takes time and, in some ways, real guts to challenge your current system with some of the ideas we have laid out and some ideas you have probably thought of in reading this chapter.

If you are ending your day and reflecting on your ability to get stuff done—particularly the most important things you needed to get done—how was e-mail a tool in doing that, and how was it a distraction? How can you make improvements so that you don't feel like you are always reacting to others' e-mail requests and demands? There are hundreds of reasons why it might not be easy to make changes in this area, because it has become ingrained in the way you work and therefore is second nature to you, but there is one big reason to make changes: improving YOUR PRODUCTIVITY and gaining back some of YOUR TIME.

Leadership Summary

E-mail is a productivity tool to allow you to communicate more efficiently:

■ Challenge inefficient e-mails that have little substance.
■ Be decisive in processing your e-mails. There are only five things (Ds) you can do with an e-mail once you have deciphered the action: Delete it, Do it, Defer it, Delegate it, or Dump (file) it.
■ Create your call to action for every e-mail you create. Be bold about that call to action: include it in the subject header.
■ Track those tasks and projects you have delegated meticulously.
■ Challenge and determine how often and when you should check e-mail. There is not a single right answer, only the next better answer for you.

Continually reengineer your e-mail practices!

PART IV

Communication Skills

CHAPTER 14

Effective Opining

A uditors frequently provide opinions. It is what we are paid to do in many cases. Most audits are performed so that an audit opinion can be provided, such as an opinion about whether financial statements are being prepared in accordance with generally accepted accounting standards, or an opinion on internal controls.

Does that make us more opinionated than non-auditors? Who knows? A personal opinion is, of course, different than an audit opinion.

An opinion, a personal one, is a belief, a view, or a judgment that is not based on empirical data or on fact. Opinions are important. They make us unique. They allow us to share our thoughts with others and provide a glimpse of how we think and what is important to us.

Are some people more opinionated than others? Sure. Is there anything wrong with that? No.

The question is, in the business world, where your opinions are important, what are the best ways to express them? **Specifically, what are the *most effective* ways to express your opinions?** What is your PROCESS for providing your opinions to others?

Also, in the business world, opinions are expressed most often in the form of advice. Opinions and advice are often interchangeable.

In many ways, we GET PAID and we GET PROMOTED based on our ability to form and express solid advice. **What is your process for providing advice?**

What Is Your Advice Process?

Have you ever thought about what your "advice process" is? Probably not formally. Let's go for it, with the objective being for you to provide the most effective advice when the situation calls for it.

What Is the Difference between Providing an Opinion and Providing Advice?

Sounds like a simple question. Opinions can be beliefs about a wide range of issues, political, religious, etc. Advice is typically providing guidance to someone else. Often, advice is *filled* with opinions. Advice is your *opinion* about how someone should proceed.

You want to provide someone with advice.

Let's start with the why question. Why do we provide people advice?

What might be the best reason to give someone advice?

Because they have asked for it!

In a best-case scenario, we provide advice to those who ask for it. We provide opinions to those who ask for them. It may be a best-case scenario, because of their willingness and desire to listen to your advice. The best time to give advice that will be HEARD is when that advice is REQUESTED.

Why do people ask for advice? (Some advice solicitors have sincere motives, and some do not.)

- *They need direction.* They need some guidance in a particular area. Maybe they are stressed or lost, and they need another point of view. Maybe they need any point of view!
- *They want to validate their own intuition.* They have an answer, but they want affirmation of their own decision (a decision that may have already been made!).
- *They want to prove themselves.* Has anyone ever asked you for your opinion on something when they already have the answer in their mind and they rebut your answer very quickly? It's a setup!

Lastly, when someone solicits your advice, in that shining moment where you know the answer and you are so excited to blurt it out that you can hardly contain yourself . . . consider not providing the answer at all! Ask yourself whether you feel that person is in a position to figure out an answer. Turn the question around, and throw it back to them. Consider having them give themselves advice. A simple "What do you think?" response, given at the right time (even when you know the single best answer) can be empowering. Don't always "give" advice, ask questions to help OTHERS find answers. Then they learn to listen to their own advice.

Providing Advice—A Generational Difference?

Older workforce generations have been more accustomed to receiving advice, even unsolicited advice, from their bosses. That was just how it was. Someone was higher than you on the organizational chart, they had more experience, and it was assumed they had more knowledge. (They usually did.) Advice, whether it was solicited or not, was provided freely and received warmly in most cases. Those same people who were so accustomed to receiving unsolicited advice are naturally more accustomed to providing it as well.

Times have changed. People are more specialized now. Younger generations feel, in many cases, that they are more knowledgeable (sometimes this is true, other times maybe not) than their older counterparts, especially in areas related to technology. They are not accustomed to receiving advice unless it is clearly visible that they need it to do their jobs better and enhance their skills. Many times, unsolicited advice is provided, but it is not needed. While older generations were okay with that, younger generations see it as a waste of time.

There is no right answer here. Neither generation is wrong or right. They are just different. We cannot change generations, and we cannot take the differences personally when dealing with people. (Every individual is different, so there is always the risk of stereotyping people solely based on their age or generational classification.) We have an opportunity to lead by understanding some of these differences. We do not have to have the right answer all the time; just being cognizant of some of these differences will serve you well in dealing with colleagues and fellow employees.

Remember, don't take it personally!

Unsolicited Advice

Of course, when people do not ASK for advice and you provide it, it is unsolicited advice. This is not always bad; sometimes it is VERY needed. It may, however, naturally be less effective because of the very fact that they did not ask for it. (They may be less likely to truly listen.)

Why do people provide unsolicited advice? There can be a number of reasons, including:

- *To feel needed and important.*

    In some situations and with some people, their need to feel important can be met by providing opinions that provide answers and fixes (in their view) to others. Providing advice gives them an outlet to feel important. This can be taken too far when a person provides advice simply to show the other person they are smarter and more knowledgeable. Many times, this type of advice can be provided in a conflicting manner.

    You have probably met some people who you feel are extremely opinionated and habitually provide unsolicited advice. They may feel the need to continually be the adviser or teacher to others. The question is, why do they act that way? If you encounter someone who acts like this, should you just blow them off? How can you act?

- *To feel important **again.***

    Some people, struggling with their own current challenges and weaknesses, can feel empowered and strengthened by telling others how to "get it done." The ironic part is they are struggling with their own issues, so they feel more comfortable providing unsolicited advice to others. (If I cannot fix my house, I'll tell you how to fix yours!)

- *Frustration about the current situation.*

    If someone sees a recurring theme in your work or in a relationship, they might just get fed up to the point where they must tell you how the problem should be solved or the situation improved.

- *The desire to help.*

    Maybe they see a very simple opportunity to help you out.

    Maybe they just discovered something new or have benefited from a way of thinking or an idea and they want to share it with you (and everyone else they meet that day).

- *Passing judgment.*

    Something you do often, or a characteristic that you have, does not sit well with them. They disagree with it, so they advise you to do things that are contrary to your practice. This situation is dicey. Judging someone in a negative way is much different from wanting to help someone improve. "Judging" advice, unless it is provided in a positive manner, is usually counterproductive to helping someone make improvements.

Strong Words, Strong Opinions

"You are wrong!"

Let's deconstruct that comment. The first word is YOU and the third word is WRONG. The "are" connects the two, and the recipient of this comment is going to identify themselves in many cases not as a person who did something wrong, but as a WRONG PERSON. Are we being too politically correct with this observation? Why can't we say someone is wrong when they are wrong? We can, and in many cases that will be fine, but no matter how tough someone may be (or may seem to be), how does telling them they are flat-out wrong help the situation? Are THEY really wrong, or do you simply have a differing opinion? It is true, in many cases, that they may just be (factually) wrong, but is your objective to prove they are wrong or to find the right answer (as a team)? Is anyone ever wrong, or are their actions, opinions, or advice not productive? There is a difference between being judgmental of a person and judging someone's actions. Make sure they know that you are addressing the actions, not the person.

"That is ridiculous!"

That's an opinion for sure, a strongly expressed one. You have probably expressed an opinion about their opinion! Maybe it is fine to talk that way to those who are close to you, but what about business colleagues you do not know well? Again, the question is, how does expressing an opinion in this manner help you with your objective?

If you are going to become a leader, do you want to be someone who disproves others' opinions?

Now maybe you never talk that way, or you do only under the right situations, but what about others around you? How can you lead change if that is the case? Get feedback! If you feel someone else is too opinionated and it is having a negative effect on the team, ask them about their view of the "opinion levels" on the team. Ask them about your opinion levels.

How do you combat too much unsolicited advice? It can be frustrating, especially in cases where it does not help you and may hurt team relationship or team dynamics.

For many, it is a lot easier to provide your own opinion than it is to listen to others' opinions. This is especially true with unsolicited advice. It is a lot easier to dish it out then it is to listen to it from someone else.

When you receive some of the unsolicited variety, consider a few points:

- *Discern between a recurring theme and a one-time event.*

  If the person providing you the advice does it all the time, then you have a behavior that should be addressed. But if it is just a rare event from this person, then consider listening intently. There may be different reasons that they are providing this advice, as we discussed earlier, and you may learn something.

- *Reflect on your actions.*

  Are you complaining a lot to them, or presenting problems? Maybe that contributes to their need to try and help?

  Consider opening a conversation with, "Bob, I am not looking for advice here, just someone to hear me out."

  Also, consider changing your behavior altogether. Ask yourself whether your actions contribute to this person's need to provide unsolicited advice frequently.

- *Reinforce "non-advice" times.*

  Proactively search and identify situations where the other person COULD have provided you advice but for whatever reason DID NOT. Then reinforce it with praise.

- *Ensure they have outlets for feedback.*

  Some people you work with may not feel that their opinions are heard, and they simply need that outlet. Formalize feedback times, or make sure they get to be heard during the planning of projects and audits.

  "Jen, talk to me about how you feel we communicate with each other. Are we too quick to jump in with advice? Are we listening to each other well?"

  "Jen, I have noticed that you have been very quick to hand out advice to me. Some of it has been helpful, but some of it has not. I want to make sure our working relationship is open enough that you have the ability to voice any concerns or opinions you have, while at the same time ensuring we're contributing to each other's productivity. Do you have any ideas on how we can improve this?"

- *Tell them it is unnecessary.*

  At some point, you need to let them know about their propensity to provide you unsolicited advice that is both unwanted and ineffective. There are soft ways to communicate this message. You will need to use what YOU are comfortable with if you are facing such a situation.

Always thank them for listening to you when you provide comments. Remember, you are providing them unsolicited advice here, too! Also, if you see an improvement in their behavior, make note of it to them quickly! Reinforce the improvement.

Below are some examples:

"I appreciate your efforts, Bob. Sometimes the advice you provide does not have the effect I bet you are looking for. Let me give you an example . . ."

"Bob, sometimes I feel like the advice you provide is not helping. Do you have a minute to talk about it?"

"Bob, I find myself getting defensive a lot and getting off track because you provide advice that I am not specifically requesting. Can we talk about that, and come up with some ideas to improve in this area?"

Your Advice Process—Tips

Someone needs your advice BADLY! How can you be most effective in providing it, especially if you are not sure the person is totally open to it? Some considerations:

- *Think about how the person will receive it.*
  The most effective frame of mind in providing advice is to think about it from the other person's perspective. Is the person naturally defensive? Is he or she naturally open to advice? What kind of emotional state is he or she in right now?
  - *What kind of advice does he or she want?* Does the person simply want a quick answer? Is he or she trying to be spoon fed? Is there a bigger issue involved? Ask questions!
  - *When is the best time to provide advice?* Is it the best time to provide it? Actually, it's not about the best time to *provide* advice; it is more about the best time for the other person to be ready to *receive and implement* the advice.
  - *What is the best style to use?* How do you change your style based on the other person? Concentrate more on how the person will receive the advice and how he or she will use it, rather than on how you will deliver it. Remember, you are the speaker; the other person has to do the harder parts—listening, consideration, and use (in some cases).

(continued)

(*continued*)

- *Ask questions.*

    Ask yourself questions in advance so that you can have a few answers BEFORE you provide the advice. Why is this person asking for advice? As discussed, maybe the other person does not need advice; maybe all he/she needs is confidence. So when the person asks for advice, or even if he or she doesn't ask for it but you feel the need to provide some, try flipping it around on them with questions such as:
    - "What do you feel is the best course of action here?"
    - "You have tackled an issue like this before . . . what did you do then?"

    Asking questions opens up the collaborative process in a nonconfrontational manner. Giving advice will be easier once you have the other person talking and both of you are COLLAB-ORATING. The advice can be provided, in time. Sometimes you will find that you will not even need to dish it out, because they dish it out before you!

- *Ask permission.*

    Advice can be permission-based. It may be more effective that way. If you ask for permission to provide the advice, you have broken down a barrier that you may not have known existed—their lack of desire to receive any advice. Permission-based advice is the next best thing to solicited advice. Some questions to consider:
    - "Can I mention an idea here?"
    - "It seems like you have uncovered a challenge here; can I provide you some advice?"
    - "Are you open to some guidance here? I believe the two of us can tackle this."
    - "Are you asking for my opinion?"

- *Challenge the need for it.*

    Why are you providing advice? Is it for the benefit of others or your team? Is it just based on frustration? Sometimes the best advice you can give is none at all.

When a man comes to me for advice, I find out the kind of advice he wants, and I give it to him.

—*Josh Billings*

Leadership Summary

Your ability to provide opinions and advice using effective methods can be a catalyst for advancement in your audit career.

Consider how to strengthen your advice process:

- How will the advice you want to deliver best be *received*?
- How can your advice be permission-based?

CHAPTER 15

Are You a Filler-holic?

"Count your uhms."

(We are auditors, we are supposed to be good at counting, right?)

If you have ever taken a public speaking class, you have probably been asked to "count your uhms." This exercise can be embarrassing, even for good speakers.

Why do people use nonwords like "er," "uhm," or "eh"? Linguists say that these are examples of word fillers. They may represent an attempt by the speaker to continue the speaking process. The speaker is telling the listener, by replacing a moment of silence with a filler, they have something more to say. Many times, we are unsure about the next thing we are going to say, or we need a moment to organize our thoughts, which creates the need for the pause—and thus for many of us, the need for a filler such as "uhm."

We all know we should avoid them. We all have been taught that "uhms" can be replaced by silence, in the form of sometimes powerful pauses.

But there are words many of us instinctively use that go way beyond these simple "uhm" fillers already discussed . . .

Conversation Word Fillers

The next time you sit down and watch television, listen to the radio, or talk to a group of people, keep track of the number of times you hear the following three phrases:

- You know
- I mean
- Like

We're not talking about using these phrases within their proper context. We are talking about extraneous words. It is amazing how many of us use these types of words when they are not needed.

Accountants are very smart people! But many of us use these words. Sometimes people will use all three phrases to start a dialogue:
"You know, I mean, like, what are we going to work on today?"

- *You know* . . .
  This phrase may be short for "Do you know what I mean?" or its slang cousin, "You know what I'm saying?" There may be good intentions in using this phrase. The speaker is trying to get buy-in to a way of thinking. Many people use this term over and over again without even realizing it. Others take it to an extreme and will end many of their sentences with the phrase, even filling a pause in the conversation with "you know?"
- *I mean* . . .
  This word may be used to clarify what you are trying to say. Eliminate it. Just say what you have to say. We know you mean it!
- *Like* . . .
  This word is sometimes used to soften comments. "There were like a hundred people trying to get into the one elevator." "Approximately" would be a much better word here—even "about" would be better than "like"!

Now, when you are watching television again, check out a sports telecast. In most sporting events, there is one sportscaster who serves as the "play-by-play guy." This person is responsible for leading the telecast.

Now check out a news program. They all have a main host or anchor.

Listen to the play-by-play guys and anchors closely. You will notice they will *rarely* use these three phrases, or any "uhms." They are smooth, they are slick, they are POLISHED speakers, and that is why they are where they are today. They are direct and to the point in their speaking.

Think of an executive at your company whom you feel excels at public speaking or is simply a good communicator. Chances are, these words are absent or nearly absent from her or his talking vocabulary.

There are literally hundreds of books on how to become a better public speaker. There are classes you can take, and some people will naturally get better as they age, because the older you get, the more you have talked in front of other people, and the more you will hear other people speak!

But if you, tomorrow, can simply **eliminate these three phrases from your vocabulary,** you will have made a simple improvement. You will sound more polished, more confident, and more to the point.

Take a closer look at your everyday language, and try and identify any frequent fillers you use beyond these three specific examples. The first thing you must do is become cognizant of your use of word fillers.

It's actually not as easy as you think. Once you are cognizant of your filler phenomenon, you will find yourself hearing these words more, and you may get frustrated because you will realize there are others around you (maybe you included) who use them constantly. If admitting you are a "filler-holic" is the first step to improved speaking, then you are on your way.

If you want to decrease your use of these fillers, here are three ideas to practice:

- If there is one filler you use more than others, such as "you know," enroll a colleague to help you with it. Tell them you are trying to improve your speech and you would like them to call you out every time you use that filler. A family member, spouse, or significant other can help, as they probably hear you talk more than anybody! It may be frustrating at first, but do not give up because you will get better if you can increase your awareness.
- Videotape or voice-record yourself for two minutes delivering a talk or simply having a casual conversation with someone else. Count the fillers and then provide the same talk again. This time try to eliminate them. All of them. Every single one.
- When you catch yourself using a filler, repeat the same thing you just said, but this time force yourself to replace the filler with a few intentional moments of silence. (Just be wary of other people who might see you talking to yourself!)

Eliminating these words forces you to be more straight-forward. It forces you to be more direct and simple. It forces you to take the time to know (and think through) what you are going to say before you say it! For many people, it causes them to slow down, and that is not always a bad thing. Do you know any people who are "stream-of-consciousness" speakers? They are basically talking at the exact same time they are thinking, sometimes even before thinking. These types may use many word fillers so that they can keep the conversation (or their part of it) going. You know?

Be wary of a "filler superiority complex." If you don't use filler words, or have now eliminated them from your speaking vocabulary, be careful about pointing out the use of fillers by others too often. Tread lightly. If you are working with a close friend, it might be fine to say, "Yes, I know" after every time they say "you know?" (so that they get the point). Say that to someone with whom you are not as close and that person will probably take offense.

Writing Word Fillers

How many auditors or accountants do you know who were English majors in college, or who were going to be English majors before deciding, at the last minute, to major in business or accounting?

Probably not that many.

Some auditors will say they majored in accounting because they had no hope of excelling in the liberal arts. In addition to speaking skills, as part of overall communication, writing skills are equally as important. There are (maybe surprisingly) a lot of strong communicators in the auditing world. Why? Maybe because we are forced to be extraverted professionally? If you are an auditor, you aren't just auditing numbers, controls, or operations; you are in many ways auditing people, and usually you work in teams. Our audit work paper files do not just contain numbers, calculations, and data files, but also explanations, conclusions, and memoranda. If you have ever had to write a persuasive memo about a very technical auditing matter, although the technical aspects and your researched evidence and theories may have been very important, the need for persuasion required solid writing skills.

Consider Writing More Than You Currently Do

Try writing every day or once a week. Maybe just a paragraph at a time. Write about anything:

- Your life
- Your leadership journey
- How you are living your mission (see Chapter 1)
- Your vision of where you are in three years and where your organization is
- How your key relationships are going, and how they can be improved
- How you see the audit profession changing
- People or events that make you mad (As we discuss in Chapter 17, sometimes it can be better to express anger on paper instead of right to the person's face.)
- A hobby
- A fictional story you create

It may provide you with a source of renewal and a creativity outlet. It may even be fun, and who knows what it will lead to down the line? How many breakthrough ideas, how many great books, how many fascinating careers have been started with a few words being written? At a minimum, it's good practice.

The audit profession is no different than others: Your communication skills, in the long run, are more of a factor in your development and advancement than your technical skills.

How do auditors improve their writing skills?

We get to the point more quickly. We communicate (in writing) in more direct ways. We lose the fillers. Word fillers are any extra words provided that are unnecessary!

Writing Tips for Auditors

Write what you understand.

If you do not understand what you are about to write, how will someone else? Make sure you can explain it in your mind or out loud before you put it in writing.

Get to the point.

Tell the reader *why* they should be reading what you have written. Tell them that quickly!

Challenge all words, sentences, and paragraphs. Less is better, as long as you are making the important points required to answer the question "why."

Keep it simple.

Short words are usually best, and can be stronger than long words. Also, use the active voice ("we reviewed the minutes") instead of the passive voice ("the minutes were reviewed by us"). "A comment was made by the auditor" is passive. "The auditor noted" is active. The active voice is compelling because it assigns agency: The action belongs to a person or persons. The passive voice is vague—who's doing that action, anyway?—and vagueness is not compelling.

(If you would like to practice identifying passive tense use, scan this book a little more closely. The author, too, needs to improve on this skill!)

Create and implement structure.

Determine the structure ahead of time. Are you writing a memo? Should there be an opening and a conclusion? Create those first. Are you going to be providing numeric data or charts in your writing? Where should they be presented?

Remember your audience.

Who will be reading this? Do you know the style they prefer? If your memo is longer than one page, will they read the whole thing? Do they like facts? Do they like specific references

(continued)

(continued)

to accounting or auditing guidance included in your memos? Not sure? Ask them! Take time to review any general comments they may have on the first piece that you prepare and they review. That may save you time in subsequent writings.

Self-edit.

Read your own writing, *out loud* if possible. While editing, remember to keep it simple. Edit your work by deleting every word that is not necessary.

Remember that spell-check does not catch everything. For example, "from" and "form" are both spelled correctly. If you mistakenly write that you "received the invoice ***form*** the accounts payable clerk," the spell checker will not help you.

Read it out loud again after you have made edits.

Do you feel like you sometimes write inefficiently? Do you ever catch yourself writing just to fill in enough space?

How do auditors improve their writing efficiency? Use your strengths. If you are like some auditors, you are:

- *A better editor than you are a writer.*

  Don't sweat the first draft! Just write it. Get it done. The quality will improve when you edit it. Extraneous words (word-fillers) are fine … in the first draft! Separate the writing process from the editing process. Make them separate tasks. If you are a good editor, you can eliminate the extraneous words, so long as you are careful to EDIT your writing every time. Soon, with practice, both tasks will take less time.

- *A better researcher than you are a writer.*

  Don't combine the two. Do your research first, and separately. Compile your notes, and then write! If you find yourself writing a memo and needing some facts or guidance you do not have, make a note, or leave a mark, but complete that reference after you are finished writing. Separate the research process from the writing process.

Leadership Summary

Get to the point. Avoid fillers in your oral and written communications. Be cognizant of extraneous fillers you use. Recognizing them is the first step toward elimination. Practice direct, simple communication, and soon you will be a more polished communicator.

CHAPTER **16**

Why We Love PowerPoint Slides

Most auditors love Microsoft PowerPoint slides. We love to use them when we are making presentations. We also love getting copies of the slides when someone else is presenting.

Why is that? Probably because we are auditors. We LOVE documentation. PowerPoint slides are loaded with all kinds of bullet points and information. We also love documentation we can take away. This way we feel if we missed something, we can always go back to the slides and remember it. PowerPoint slides represent proof that a presentation was made.

No doubt you've attended a public conference where the presenter has slides, but the audience was not provided with a hard copy. What is one of the most predictable questions an audience member will ask? You know the answer: "Where can we get a copy of these slides?"

What Is Your Objective in Making a Presentation?

PowerPoint slides are OVERRATED.
   The goals of an effective presentation are:

- To convey a point
- To enroll the participants into a way of thinking
- To help the audience learn new skills

The goal is NOT to cram in as many bullet points of information as humanly possible. A presentation is not meant solely to provide written information. If that is all you are aiming to do, then all we need to do is give them your notes and slides copies, or videotape your lecture and throw it on the Internet.

Recently, I attended an alumni event for one of the "Big" accounting firms. One of the partners presented information about FAS 157. Even if you don't know what this financial accounting standard is, you can probably imagine what the presentation was like . . . and you would be right. (It was dry.) This particular partner was very articulate and a polished speaker, but that was all she did—speak, and most of her speaking was repeating the exact words on the slides. It is interesting to think what would have happened had the slides been taken away from her. In this case, the speaker might have been able to adjust, because she really knew her stuff! However, many speakers would have struggled. Many speakers work through their content by simply working through bullet-point slides. Have you ever been in a presentation where the speaker simply reads off of his slides in a monotone way that causes you to fall asleep? Sometimes it's apparent the speaker would not even make it through the presentation without the aid of his slides. The slides are the presentation.

Have you ever been leading a presentation or watched someone else lead a presentation where one slide is out of order and then it takes more than a few seconds for the presenter to figure out exactly what was supposed to be said next? They may appear flustered. That is a "slide-dependent" presentation.

The accounting industry is full of presentations made with zillions of PowerPoint slides, and you will see bullet point after bullet point of information. Many of us have been doing this for years, and we are comfortable with it! I have heard people say that if they have a lot of time to fill they are much more prepared if they have more than enough slides to get through it.

However, there needs to be a change, and many presenters are starting to do that. Some good ones have been doing it for years. The younger generations, who are truly integrated into all new forms of technology, are more accustomed to learning in varying ways. They require a much more interactive, much richer multimedia type of presentation to command their attention.

The other thing that numerous slides do is make your presentation rigid. You have less flexibility in making your points. You have less flexibility in allowing the audience to make their points, if every single point and answer is embedded in the presentation slides, using your specific language. It limits conversations, and it limits exploration time where presenter and audience members find answers together.

Present with the Audience in Mind

Instead of focusing on slides as the basis for your presentation, consider some other ideas.

- *Use stories*
    People love stories, and they remember them.

- *Use images*

    A presentation slide that uses a single picture or image, rather than words, will push the onus of the work from the slide to the presenter and the message. Think about it this way: If one presenter makes a solid point by reading off a bunch of bullet points, and another makes a point and says pretty much the same thing but uses a very good image as the slide, which one do you think you will remember better?

    I once attended a presentation in which the speaker was telling a story about some auditing work that had been done on a trial balance. They had tested the file thoroughly. He had one slide up with a picture of the detailed trial balance. Then once he was done talking about the testing, he showed the second slide, which had the bottom of the trial balance blown up and you could just see two numbers—the debits and the credits. They did not match: Most of the testing was a waste of time, and written on the slide next to the numbers that did not match was a "WTF?" in red ink. We will not interpret that abbreviation here, but the audience laughed out loud. Only two slides. No bullet points. The audience, including me, remembers.

- *Use videos*

    There is a reason YouTube was sold for more than a billion dollars. One point here—there does seem to be a generational gap in the use of videos. Older generation auditors typically feel that if you are going to use a video, it must be professionally created—and sometimes they can go overboard in the production, especially if it is being shown to younger employees, who prefer real-life-type videos as seen on YouTube. Think about your audience. Think about what resonates with them, not what resonates with you. It is not always the same. Not sure? Ask them. Involve them.

- *Ask questions of the audience!*

    Asking questions, especially during a formal presentation, is a skill that can be practiced and improved.

- *When the audience asks questions, focus first on listening to their questions instead of going right to the answer.*

    Ensure that not only you can hear the question, but everyone else can also. Make a big deal of that. If there is a microphone available (in the case of large groups) see if the "asker" can be given one so everyone can hear. If the audience is very large, repeat the question so everyone can hear it. If the question is ambiguous to you, make sure you ask a question of the person to gain a better understanding. Have them clarify it for you. If needed, rephrase the same question and ask for their confirmation that you do truly understand it. Remember they are part of the show. Make them feel important, really important. Taking the time to ensure you understand the question makes them feel important. Getting them a microphone so that everyone can hear also makes them feel important. Get crazy and throw some of their questions back to the audience. See if others might have answers. Sometimes the person asking the question might have an answer.

Note that none of the tips above focused on slides. They focused on using a more interactive approach with different media and involving the audience as much as possible.

Preparing a Presentation with Purpose

Slides, if needed, should reinforce your message, your stories, and your discussions. That's all. The slides should not be the show—the presenter and the audience should be the show. Make your audience the show. They will remember that.

If you are putting together a presentation, try the following:

- *Throw away your slides* (or at least put them to the side)!
- *Create a mission statement for your presentation.*

  What message do you want the audience to take with them? Be specific and as clear as you can be. Ask yourself: *What is the one thing I would like them to remember or learn?* Then focus on that as much as possible. Make sure you mention that at least five times in your presentation.

  I was lucky to have recently attended a childbirth class where I listened to a very entertaining and effective pediatrician provide us some advice about early childrearing. His main message, something he said no less than 12 times during his 30-minute presentation: Feed them and they will grow. Read to them and they will be smart. His presentation was very good. (By the way, he did not use one PowerPoint slide, unlike his earlier counterparts.) He was memorable, so much so that when my wife and I decided to pick a pediatrician, we went with his group. In our first appointment with him, he actually asked us, "What did you remember from that class?" My wife blurted out before I had a chance to say anything, "Feed them and they will grow. Read to them and they will be smart." If he had simply buried that message in some PowerPoint slide in his presentation, how do you think things may have gone? We may have never signed up for him to be our baby's doctor, and we never would have remembered his mission statement!

- *Create the presentation outline first.*

  THEN figure out the best methods to present your ideas, and try using some variety.

- *Plan to grab their attention.*

    Ask yourself how you will get the audience involved and grab their attention in the first 30 seconds. This does not mean getting their attention by talking about your illustrious background. It means you need to talk about them or talk about something they can relate to in a quick manner.

- *Limit your slide use.*

    Try not to have more than two bullet points per slide, and try not to have too many words per bullet point. I know that sounds tough. Really tough if you are going to use PowerPoint slides. Remember the slides are not the show; you and the audience are the show. The slides should merely reinforce your points.

Leadership Summary

Have we mentioned the main point enough?

The slides are not the show. You and the audience are the show.

When you are making a presentation, help the audience to remember you, to remember themselves, and to remember your message.

CHAPTER 17

One Way to Avoid Office Rage

Have you ever been in a situation where something happened or somebody did something that had you about to blow a fuse? Consider these examples:

- An executive, once again, pushed you hard to meet a deadline to get some work papers complete for their review on a certain day and time. The deadline came. You personally sacrificed, big time, to make it happen. You worked long hours and so did your team. After a lot of hard work, you were ready. Then after all that, the partner did not show up for their review (or the work papers sat in their virtual inbox for days). You are frustrated!

- A staff person told you that you were wrong about how the client used an accrual account. The person said it in a very combative way right in front of the rest of the team, undermining your authority. You had talked to this person just the other day about the issue of expressing differences in professional ways. You are mad!

- A client blatantly told you one thing about a desired deadline and then said something totally different to your colleagues. You are confused and mad!

- Your manager yelled at you in front of your face and other partners. Talk about disrespect and a lack of professionalism!

Your Confrontation Style?

Some people, in the middle of these types of situations, will try and get a handle on their emotions first. They will talk or vent to a friend they can confide in or their spouse instead of charging into the "offender's" office.

Some people are not confrontational, and although the issue hurts and possibly affects their productivity, the awkwardness of confronting the other person is too intolerable for them to do anything about it.

Some people will just jump down the offender's throat.

If you spend just a little time reflecting, I bet you can uncover your natural disposition or style when it comes to confrontation. Are you more apt to avoid confrontation, jump right into it, or be somewhere in the middle? There is no right or wrong style; there is just your style, your degree of comfort with confrontation. Those who are more comfortable with confrontations will typically be more prone to welcome it and will "mix it up" more quickly. Those who are on the other end of the spectrum will typically avoid confrontations at all costs.

No matter which side of the spectrum you are on, if you find yourself in a situation where you are flat-out emotionally peeved (whether you are comfortable with confrontation or not), try this:

Get out everything you have to say **in writing.** Draft an e-mail or letter. Let it flow. Get it all out. Be rude, be emotional, dare we say it . . . **be hateful.**

It will probably be one of the fastest written letters you have ever created. **Just don't send it.**

Let it sit in your drafts folder, and make sure you never put the addressee's e-mail address in the TO: section or accidentally hit the SEND button. If you handwrote it, let it sit in your drawer; just make sure the drawer stays locked!

The exercise of expressing how you feel will probably, by itself, make you feel a little bit better. But that might not be enough.

Now you need to wait. Wait a few hours, maybe a day, maybe longer, if that is what it takes. If you still feel anger, go ahead and add to your manuscript. Make sure you have everything out of your head and your heart and it's now on paper. That should provide you some temporary peace. Then, as we said, sit on it.

Let it go, for a while. Revisit the document after your emotions have subsided. Read it.

If you have waited long enough, it will probably feel *less* emotional now.

Maybe you will read through it again and say to yourself that it does not bother you anymore. Maybe, just maybe, you will feel like you overreacted, and the issue will be done right there. There's an art to letting something go, to understanding that, in the big picture of things, what had you really mad is not a big deal.

However, in many cases, if something had you that fired up, chances are that the issues are deep-rooted, and you have a problem you need to resolve. This problem may be hurting your attitude and productivity, which affects not only you but your teams and company as well.

If you believe in the "law of attraction," when we allow our emotions to get the best of us, we tend to attract others who do the same, resulting in more of those types of situations. The opposite can be true, also. If we can keep our emotions in check under tough circumstances and use more logic in our interactions with others and in our decision making, then maybe we'll attract people who do the same.

So, who and what are you attracting?

Turn Anger into Problems and Solutions

Now let's read your manuscript so you can use a more logical approach to solving that problem.

Get to the root of the problem, not the person.

Think about the **actions and results** that are bothering you. Add notes on the side as you read it. You will probably be amazed at how much of the letter is simply the expression of emotions. Sift through those emotions and identify the **issues** that caused your (almost) outburst.

Answer the following questions:

1. What can be done to change the current situation?
2. How can I think about the issues from the other person's point of view? (This will only be possible if you have let a lot of your anger go.)
3. What suggestions can I make that will facilitate change? (Make sure the suggestions are about the team, that they are not one-sided, and that they include some actions YOU will take to help.)
4. What are the benefits to my company and/or the person it is directed at, if this change occurs?

If you can answer these questions, you can create a real action plan.

Don't totally *dismiss* the emotional side of this, though. The key to this approach lies in not MAKING action decisions or taking actions while your emotions are getting the best of you.

Now that you have created a reasoned action plan, you can still talk from the heart. When you are ready to make your case, tell the person this issue unsettled you and affected your work. Don't dismiss the emotional roller-coaster you just went through. You may even want to say that it affected you so much that you sat down and formally created a plan to improve the situation.

Before you approach the "offender," try this: Write a second letter, but this time, make it a script of the key points you are going to say.

Take your edited outburst letter where you extracted out the specific problems and unwanted actions and use it to help create your script. Make sure to answer the four questions noted.

It's time to have your sit-down with the other person. But there's one more thing to consider.

Do you have a very important discussion coming up with somebody in your life? Do you feel nervous about it? Script what you will say. The conversation may not go "as scripted," but the act of preparing a script will allow you to remember your important points and usually put you more at ease in advance of your talk.

Afraid of feeling "scripted" when you talk to the "offender"? Practice in front of a friend. If it's a really important matter, it's worth the investment of your time. You will both learn a lot!

Get the other person talking first. Consider asking some questions to elicit their thoughts. Script the questions. Maybe it's a good time to ask for feedback on your performance? Maybe you simply come straight out and ask them about the situation. Ask them what they thought about what happened.

It may be better, in cases where you have a real agenda, to begin by getting that other person to start talking. In a case like this, it makes the meeting less one-sided and it may get some of the exact issues that you would like to discuss out in the open—but now they are "outed" by the other person.

If that happens, you can respond to what *the other person* has brought up. **In short, it has become a team cause instead of a one-person crusade.**

Remember, your agenda can be based on assumptions, too. Make sure you first seek to understand the other person's point of view. Then you will have the entire picture, and you will be fairer in making points that consider BOTH perspectives. In short, you will be a leader of a team effort in your response, not just a one-person wrecking crew only looking out for yourself.

The discussion, if handled correctly, should be less about your agenda and your demands and more about uncovering problems and coming up with solutions. Demands are rigid and one-sided. Solving problems allows for many solutions, creativity, and teamwork.

Using this conflict resolution approach may help you make a quantum leap in the personal growth of your leadership skills.

If you can somehow keep the documents somewhere safe, retain them—*both* of them. A few years later, if you read those documents again, you will look back fondly on them, especially that first emotional outburst manuscript!

You will naturally ask yourself: What would have happened if I sent this first letter instead of executing the second one? What would have happened had you not done any reflecting, but instead simply reacted emotionally and quickly to the situation? If you are someone who avoids conflict, what would have happened had you clammed up and withdrawn from the situation and not stood up for yourself?

Being angry is a natural human emotion, but uncontrolled emotional aggression in the workplace never helps the situation. It may make you feel temporarily better, because you felt like you were standing up for yourself, which you *should* do. But if you can take a step back, get control of your emotions, and act in a way that serves both parties' interests, you are well on your way to becoming a LEADER. If you wanted to avoid the situation altogether because of your fear of conflict, this method might help you tackle the issue head-on in a less confrontational way.

Leadership Summary

In those (hopefully rare) cases where another person's actions have you on the verge of an emotional rage or withdrawal, challenge yourself to:

- Reflect on your anger BEFORE you let it get the best of you.
- Find an outlet for expressing your emotions. Do not dismiss your emotions. Extract what is bothering you, and define the PROBLEM that needs to be fixed. Turn anger into problems, and then you can search for solutions.
- If, after your reflection, you still feel the problem needs a solution, confront the "offender." Focus on actions. Don't make it personal. Make it an opportunity for growth for both of you.
- Consider writing all of this on paper! Document your "anger," the extracted problems, some potential solutions, even the discussion you need to have.

PART V

Client Relationship Skills

CHAPTER 18

Who Is the Puppet Master?

C lients pull our strings.

They tell us when we can come out in the field to perform the audit.

They tell us when THEY are ready to provide us with accounting records.

They tell us where we can work at their offices.

They tell us when we can show up daily and when we can leave.

They tell us who we can talk to and when. **We've even heard stories about clients who told the auditors when they could use the bathroom!** Seriously.

Obviously, this is not the case on all audits, and certainly not on all of your audits, but you can probably relate.

We all have experienced one case, for example, where our office conditions at the audit site were not ideal. Have you ever worked in what really was a janitor's supply closet at one of your clients? Have you ever worked in a dark, dingy basement where you weren't sure if the ground was moving or if you needed to bring a big can of Raid with you the next day? Did you see the 1999 movie *Office Space*? Remember Milton's last office, down in the basement? Was that scene even funnier because you could relate?

Who Is Pulling the Strings?

Have you ever heard a fellow auditor say or joke, "My job would be easy if I did not have to deal with clients. I could get so much work done without them!"

If you had to identify, right now, whether you or your client were pulling more of the strings in your relationship, who would it be?

The important thing is not defining one party or the other as the puppet master. It's what all this one-sided string-pulling results in.

Under this scenario, because it's the auditee, not the audit expert (you), who is in charge of many aspects of the actual audit, the results will be

inefficient audits and **subpar client service.** These are results neither party desires.

The Single Biggest Opportunity to Improve Your Audit?

What if you were to ask an audit partner at your firm how he or she would feel if you could manage your audit clients in a way that would result in:

- The client proactively reaching out to you when significant accounting issues arose
- All accounting records and client-prepared items being provided accurately, completely, and on time
- The client's personnel being readily available to answer any questions your team needs answered
- The client completing all close-out items, such as representation letters or follow-up on legal letters

Second, ask the same partner what kind of an effect such a scenario would have on the firm's realization rates, profits, partners' pay, and—**this is the kicker and you have to ask it**—the firm's ability to provide higher compensation and advancement opportunities to its professionals, such as YOU.

How would that partner respond?

We have asked partners at auditing firms these two questions. Their answer usually starts with a hearty chuckle but then is followed by a curious look and a question, such as "How are you going to do that?" Their interest overrides their initial skepticism.

Now, the perfect client management scenario, as outlined, may never happen, but that does not diminish the opportunity that awaits you. If you can improve client management on many of your engagements, the results will be staggering. From a financial standpoint, this can be the *biggest opportunity* to improve your audit. This point is not only true for external financial auditors, either. Internal auditors, IT auditors, and all other types of auditors face the same challenges in managing their (internal) clients, *and have the same opportunities* to save time and costs.

Let's explore some ways we can improve client management in the sections that follow.

Stop Managing "Clients"

Auditors like to use the term *client management*. It typically refers to the time and effort we spend in getting the client to be audit-ready and audit-accommodating. It's a buzzword for us.

"Let's do a better job of managing the client this year."

We have all been in a situation in which we felt that managing a particular audit client was almost a lost cause. While some clients are naturally easier to get along with and manage than others, the ability to manage them more effectively is a real skill that can be acquired and always improved. If you take one tough client and gave it to three separate audit teams, would the results be exactly the same? Probably not.

> How do you separate your personal time management from client management?
>
> You can't! Problems arise when you think the two are separate issues.
>
> Sometimes, we do not realize the impact our clients have on our own time management. You can improve your personal time management, priority management, and energy management skills all you want, but if you do not manage your clients well, they will have an impact on everything else you do. Client and personal time management are intertwined.

Many times, we just assume a client is going to be difficult because that is what we have come to expect. We volunteer to have the audit run on their terms, because we are not willing to do much about it, or we have come to see it as inevitable.

With our most challenging clients, the first thing we should focus on changing is our own attitudes. Do not let prior years' experiences sour your outlook. If you have never audited a particular client before, do not let assumptions about the type of organization under audit sour your outlook. Keep in mind that if you have a negative attitude toward that client, and *you want that client to change*, will that attitude be effective in getting that change, that improvement, to happen?

It's not a lost cause. You are in charge. You can lead the positive change. Let's roll on!

The first problem with the subject of client management might simply be the actual term. Do we really manage *clients*?

The answer is an emphatic **no,** which may help us see why so many auditors struggle in this area.

What is a client? A client is a business or an organization. But that entity is made up, first and foremost, of the people running it.

We don't manage clients, we manage people, and to do that in better ways, we should think of client management as managing individuals at the entity you are auditing.

"Next year, I am going to do a better job of asking the client for their schedules and supporting documentation earlier."

That sounds like a great goal; however, it makes the fatal assumption that you are asking "clients." You are going to be asking for these items from specific individuals at client organizations, and asking for the client assistance items earlier might be the worst thing you could do when dealing with a particular person. It really depends on the person, and as such, you will need to adjust your client management based on the particular person or people involved.

Dale Carnegie, in his book *How to Win Friends and Influence People*, offers us some advice in his timeless quote:

> *There is only one way under high water to get anybody to do anything. And that is by making the other person want to do it.*

To make someone want to do something, you must first understand more generally what they "want." If you subscribe to the theory that the best way to serve a client, even an audit client, is to first understand their needs, then you first must uncover those needs. Also, be open to the idea

Born to Be Skeptical

This is crazy. I am an auditor. I perform a specific function. I do not have the time or desire to be getting all "mushy" with my clients. I perform a high-quality audit and that is all I need to do.

If you see yourself only as the "auditor," that is how your clients will see you, also. What if you view yourself as a professional services provider? Is that just a play on words? Maybe, but let's clarify what the difference might be and why it might matter.

An auditor performs an audit, and while completing the audit is your team's number-one goal (whether you are on a team of one or a very large team), if your clients, when they think about you and your team, only see you as an audit opinion, that is all you will be. You are a commodity, and they merely need you to sign off on the commodity (i.e., audit) you provide. Therefore, in the clients' eyes, that is the ONLY benefit you provide and the only role in which they will see you.

However, if they view you as more than that, as someone who helps them solve problems, then they will see you as more than an auditor. They will see you as a solutions provider.

that your client—or more importantly, the individual people with whom you will be dealing—will not simply have business needs, but other (maybe more personal) needs, also, you will be on your way.

If you hold negative feelings toward a particular person at a client organization, guess what? News flash—that person can tell, and that situation helps to produce mutual (negative) feelings.

Auditing is a very personal business. We get to know the clients we work with very well. We have to. The challenge lies in dealing with the people (1) with whom you do not naturally get along and/or (2) who are very difficult to manage in ways so that you obtain all the information you need to conduct an efficient (and effective) audit.

So let's talk about the tough situations.

The Client Sees Us as a Necessary Evil

Clients sometimes see us as the outside folks who make their life harder. Maybe this is how a particular client sees all auditors. Maybe auditors have given them some good reasons in the past to feel that way. That doesn't matter now.

You must be able to see the good in each of the people with whom you work at the client organization. The biggest challenge will be in doing so with those people in whom "the good" is not obvious. Maybe a lot of people do not get along with a certain individual at the client. It's really easy to just be like everyone else. But think: *Everyone* has a good part to them. The challenge is for you to find out what that part is in this person. Everyone has potential to improve, even your worst clients. You just have to help THEM realize that potential. The easiest way to do that? Do what probably few other people have done. Become curious. Become observant. Continually search for what they are good at, and praise them for it.

> Leadership is unlocking people's potential to become better.
>
> —*Bill Bradley*

In what ways has this person communicated well with you?
What items has this person provided to you on time?
What insightful information has this person shared with you?
If you are on the lookout, you will be able to identify some of these things the person has done, and once you have identified those things, you can PRAISE them! You can reinforce the good in that person, the potential he or she has to deliver. Then see if that does not spur the person to try and replicate his or her actions and gain more praise.

The Client Is Incompetent in Getting Ready for the Audit

You have probably worked with some clients in the past who were the nicest people, but they did not deliver what they were tasked to as part of the audit. That is a different kind of challenge, but the result is the same. Then there are other clients who are both difficult to work with *and* (in your opinion) incompetent.

You are an internal or external auditor facing a scenario where the client struggles mightily to be audit-ready. The question for you becomes, "How can the client develop the skills necessary to get better?" Part of it may be that they do not understand what an audit is; we talk a bit about client education in Chapter 19. Part of it is buy-in. Have they "bought in" to what needs to be done on their side for an audit to happen? Executive buy-in needs to happen. What can you do so that the leadership at the client organization (1) understands their lack of preparation, (2) understands how that lack of preparation affects THEM, and (3) decides to make a change?

Try something crazy next year. Ask the client for feedback on how you, together, can resolve the client management problems. There are probably things *both* parties can do. How do you start that conversation? Consider soliciting feedback on yourself and on your team. Ask THEM how improvements can be made and how that will positively affect THEM. Listen to what they have to say. Listen intently. (If you want to read more about soliciting feedback, skip back to Chapter 3 right now.) **Ensure that executive leadership is part of this discussion** ... on both sides!

Also, if you are an external auditor, remember that keeping the client can be challenged altogether. Sometimes you just have to let go. This may be a difficult issue to consider if you are not a manager or partner at your firm. You probably feel like you have no say in the situation. But it is possible that you can ask a few questions of the partner to get her or him THINKING:

- What are the characteristics of a client that we seek when engaging them?
- What are our protocols when they do not deliver what they are supposed to deliver?
- Tell me how we would choose to terminate a client relationship. What would happen?
- Am I crazy in wondering why we have chosen to be engaged by this client?
- What realization are we getting on this client?
- What is the cost to our team of having to deal with them?

The First Step in Client Management

Client management requires **client management *planning.*** Let's say that one more time in a different way: Improved client management requires client management planning.

It has been said that the definition of insanity is doing the same thing over and over and expecting different results. Therefore, **if we desire to have a better managed client, then we must *plan* not to do the same thing we did last year.** That is a little bit different from many of the comments we have heard from audit teams over the years, such as:

"Next year we will do a better job of getting the client ready earlier."

"We'll ask for the client assistance items earlier."

Those may be well-intentioned goals or objectives, but they do not formally and specifically tell us how and when we are going to do these things. Without details, without specific plans, those are "pie in the sky" goals.

The term *planning* means a lot of different things to different audit firms and audit teams.

However, many different audit "plans" lack what can be the single most important consideration that can determine the success of the audit: a formal plan to manage the client.

When asked to respond to how Lance Armstrong, seven-time winner of the Tour de France, continually destroyed his competition, Nancy Jenkins of the *Washington Post*, responded,

> *No other rider goes out into the Alps and rehearses the big climbs with a heart monitor and computer readout, analyzes the output, and then rides it again and again until he hits the numbers he wants. That's what Lance does. He knows the percentage of every grade, and what his heart rate and cadence should be, and for how long, if he wants to win the stage. No one else weighs their food either. His preparation is what has killed them. He always says, he wins the Tour in December, not July. (Washington Post Express, July 26, 2005)*

When do you win the battle to better manage your client?

Is it the first day you get out to the client after the (audit cut-off) period ends? Is it when we are ready to start field work? Whether it is a financial statement audit, operational audit, or whatever, that may be too late.

If we think of each separate audit as a race, we must proactively plan to win that race by creating a strategy, creating action steps, and holding ourselves accountable for completing such steps, and doing this as EARLY as needed.

Try something new on your next client engagement where improved client management represents a good opportunity: Write down the opportunity.

Write down the negative impacts that occurred last year when things went awry (if it is a recurring audit). Write down how you would like the audit to go, from a client management perspective, this year. Be bold and audacious in your thinking. Write down the ideal scenario. What you have done is identify a *gap*, and now you can take the time to brainstorm ways to fill the gap to get closer to where you want to be.

Time-block an hour (or more) and brainstorm specific ideas and action steps you can do this year to improve your approach. **Make it a team project if you can!**

But don't forget to consider the individuals who will be helping you! Write down their names. Write next to their names what you know about them. Yes, write down their quirks.

Obviously the closer your relationship with the client employees, the easier this will be. When you think of ideas, **think of those people.** Maybe you cannot "connect" with every single person at your client organization, but you can continually learn about them. Those people need to know they (the individuals) are an integral part of an efficient and effective audit process. Consider documenting the key characteristics that you learn about the key individuals you will be collaborating with on the audit.

How cool would it be to transition an annual audit to a new team and be able to provide them with this information? Passing along your "quirky" knowledge? Some auditors do that informally already within their organization, when one (transitioning) auditor talks to the new auditors who are taking over within that organization. Consider formalizing it on all recurring audits. Maybe you can call it the client "rap sheet"!

Some items to consider capturing in your documented client management plans:

- Who are the key personnel at the client organization?
- What problems did we encounter last year (if applicable)? What was the negative impact on the audit of these problems? How did they affect the client?
- If we could paint a perfect scenario this year in which this problem is rectified, how would that scenario work?
- What do we know about the key client personnel? What are their characteristics? Their quirks? Their hobbies? Their challenges? Which people on our team have the best relationships with them?
- How do we improve our relationship with the individuals at the client in the coming year (or shorter period)?

■ What are some crazy, outlandish ideas that we have (ALL) brainstormed to help us manage the client better this year? Next, what are the feasible and practical ideas that we can implement? What is our deadline for implementing them? Who will do what? Why do we feel like these methods will work on *this particular* client? (How are we aligning our ideas to the unique individuals?)

Stop "Managing" Clients

We challenged the word *client* before; now let's challenge the word *management*. Management, as defined by dictionary.com, refers to "the act or manner of managing; **handling, direction, or control.**"

Control? We couldn't control our clients even if we wanted to. There is a better word here, also.

It's **collaboration.** Collaboration is much more two-way than management. One synonym for collaboration is *coaction*; another is *teamwork.*

It's not us versus them. It's just *us*. Sure, we have different roles, and the auditor's role is based on independence, but we both want the same simple outcome: to complete a great audit.

If we want collaboration, if we want teamwork, if we want to encourage coactions from the clients ... we need to start with ourselves.

We must build **rapport.** You do that by building a relationship. You do that by *showing* the client that you want to help them, and not just their company. You can really excel by your desire and follow-through in helping them *personally*. Business is personal. We do business with people we like, **and we do business more efficiently and effectively with people with whom we have built up rapport.** If someone knows deep down that you want him or her to succeed personally, then that is contagious. It's less about the auditors getting their PBCs faster. It is more about that individual, who knows you support them, getting you the PBCs in a way that will help you out.

> I suppose leadership at one time meant muscles; but today it means getting along with people.
>
> —*Mohandas K. Gandhi*

The best time to start building rapport is when you first meet someone. If you already know the person, the best time to build rapport is when you don't need anything from him or her. It sounds simple, huh? *But how often do you think about your clients when YOU DON'T HAVE TO?*

Auditors have so many talents, so many resources we don't even realize. If we get to know our clients on a personal level and LISTEN to them, we can help them in so many ways.

What would it take for you to think about your client during the off-season? What will it take for you to build more rapport?

Is it proactively scheduling a lunch with your contact there, every so often? You have been to lunch with clients in less stressful times before, you know how much fun they can be, and you know how they allow you to let the details of the audit go and talk about good big-picture issues. You get to learn more about them personally. You are both more at ease.

Is creating a two-hour routine in your schedule, once every two weeks, during which you can connect with "off-season" clients an idea worth pursuing? Maybe you can spend some time in just THINKING about your clients. This may be time well spent. You are thinking about the client and their business, not just the audit. That is because you are not performing the audit now. You are simply pushing yourself to think about them when you don't have to do so.

Born to Be Skeptical

What about those one-time audits we perform? The client is nonrecurring. Why would I think about or try to assist those clients when I am not auditing them? I may never see them again. I do not have time to think about them!

Surprise them. Call them a few weeks or months after the audit and see how they are doing. You do not have time? If you make it a routine, the time will already be allocated in your schedule. There may always be time constraints. The question is: Is it a priority? The next question is: Can you see how kick-butt client management can allow you to have MORE time? Can you see how adding value to clients, even those you might not see again, will make that a consistent part of how you work as an auditor? Clients will SEE that attitude and want to respond in kind. Who knows ... maybe a client contact who thought he or she would never see you again will call you up or help you out in some way that surprises you! Why can't a "client" become part of your social capital? As we discussed in Chapter 5, you can strengthen one of your most important assets, your social capital, by strengthening others, including your clients. Even the one-time clients!

And by the way, if you proactively do some of these things, and institute your own creative ideas, you will feel something lift from your back, too. You know what that is?

Those nasty puppet strings.

Leadership Summary

Better client management, a huge opportunity on almost every audit, requires intentional client management planning. Get the entire audit team involved.

Clients can be better managed when:

- You don't see them as "clients," but individuals.
- You don't see it as "management," but collaboration between two partners with the same cause (an efficient audit).
- You take the time to get to know the specific personnel, and you look for ways to help them, both personally and professionally. You build rapport!

CHAPTER 19

What Hat Are You Wearing?

"You are the auditor, you tell me."
"That is what we hire you for!"
"Shouldn't you have caught that?"
"When you are here, that's when we get around to fixing those things."
"We do not have time to do those things. Just get it done."

How Many Hats Are You Wearing?

Auditors are very conscientious professionals. We do whatever we feel it takes to get the job done on time and to meet high-quality standards. **But sometimes we do too much!** Sometimes we perform too many functions. We wear our auditor's hat, but we wear a lot of other hats, as well.

Do clients take advantage of our conscientious ways? Sometimes. Performing an audit and forming an audit opinion requires one very basic, almost ridiculous sounding assumption: *the bookkeeping, accounting (or IT systems work), and audit preparation must be done first.*

I am sure you are saying, "Of course it does."

If you are an external auditor, go grab a client engagement letter and read the terms. It surely includes stipulations about the client supplying all records and the accounting being the responsibility of the client, not the auditors. If you are an internal auditor you have something similar.

Clients get us to do a lot of work that is not included in the real scope of an audit. Some examples include:

- Closing their books
- Preparing audit schedules

If we are helping them to close the books and prepare the accounting estimates, then we are AUDITING our own work! First, you must be wary of independence violations.

Recent new auditing standards help us with this cause. Many of the rules preclude us from performing certain functions. That technical guidance can be found in other literature.

There are actually four (or more) "hats" an auditor may wear during the course of completing an engagement: the bookkeeper hat, the accounting hat, the audit preparation hat, and the auditor hat. The first three hats are supposed to be worn only by the client.

AT A MINIMUM, if you are going to wear more than just the audit hat then you must make sure they understand that you are wearing additional hats—and therefore doing extra work!

Audit Your Audits

What tasks did your team perform in the different roles? Most important, what are the specific things your team did that were beyond what an auditor should do? To decipher what these nonaudit tasks are, you must talk about this as a team BEFORE the audit. Once the audit is underway, it may be too late. The team must agree that this is important and that everyone commits to tracking the nonaudit time and effort.

It takes time to track time!

Some audit teams who track their time document it as part of their budget to actual "time-tracking."

Now you have the "work done beyond the audit scope" results ... documented.

Client Education

Make sure the client understands that you are wearing additional hats!

If you have audited your audits, and you know what tasks you performed that were outside of your typical audit scope, then you have specific examples to provide to the client when educating them. You need to educate them. Most clients have little real knowledge of what an audit is and what it isn't. They believe an audit is something that must be done, and in many cases, they believe the auditors do basically everything that "needs to get done." Not true. We perform an audit. That is all.

You must remember that clients are conditioned this way, and you have probably contributed to their conditioning. You (or another auditing shop or team) did all this stuff in previous years, so they expect you to continue to do it.

To combat this conditioning, some auditors have:

- Created client education seminars
- Allocated time in client planning meetings to simply educate the client on the role(s) of the auditor and auditee

What ideas do you have? What ideas does your team have? And, what ideas does your organization have?

Born to Be Skeptical

How can I get the client to do more than they are accustomed to doing?

We can educate them all we want, but if they do not change their ways, how was that worth it? We have been performing some of our audits this way for years. Other audits involve clients who DON'T WANT to be audited in many ways.

You can't make anyone do anything, as we have discussed. They have to want to do it.

So, if the "education" does not do the trick by itself, maybe you should start by asking them some questions:

- How do we get these specific schedules completed next year? (Provide them examples of the schedules.)

   If they say that you, the auditor, did them last year, then make the point that these are not "auditor" schedules. Consider helping them to complete them for the first time. This is time well spent!
- How can we get enrollment from your folks on these ideas to make the audit more efficient next year? (Be sure to include not just what they will need to do, but what you plan to do to make it more efficient as well.)

Create your own (powerful) questions. Lead the change. Keep at it.

New clients, or clients who are part of one-time audits, represent an opportunity: You can educate them to understand an auditor's role from the beginning. Educate them as part of your planning. Ensure that they understand the hats you will wear and the hats you will not—indeed, cannot—wear. In doing so, inquire about how you can wear your "auditor's hat" in the most efficient manner for them.

An engagement letter with standard generic language about the client's responsibilities is typically not enough! You must ensure that the most important individual people know specifically what is required of your team and of them. Be creative. Create an audit road map. Tie it to anticipated deadlines and milestones the audit team (or the client) may have. If, for example, the client has an anticipated deadline for the completion of the audit, tie the critical fulfillment of their role to that deadline they have requested.

Leadership Summary

Ensure that your teams and your clients understand the role of an auditor and the role of a client. Why? Because this understanding ensures independence and assists you in running more efficient audits. Wearing multiple hats at the same time is inefficient!

If you feel like you are wearing "too many hats" for a particular client, consider tracking the time and effort put into each of the different roles (hats) and then communicate that information to your executive(s) and to the client. Educate your clients to understand the respective roles of client and auditor, and work with them to enhance the roles to result in a more efficient audit.

CHAPTER 20

Be Memorable

M any organizations institute policies designed to help the organization excel in customer service. A few common examples:

- Employees will return all calls within 24 hours.
- Employees are expected to look neat and clean.

These types of generic policies may have good intentions, but they seem more like a form of "compliance" with minimum standards, and they definitely do not inspire auditors to provide MEMORABLE client service.

Do auditors think about memorable client service? Sometimes? Perhaps at an annual meeting? Maybe after one of the executives has come back from a seminar on client service? Let's take it a lot further now.

Remind Clients of Your Value

One way to be memorable: Remind people about you and your team!

How well you feel you and your team did the job pales in comparison to the client's perception of the job you did. Remember, sometimes their perception is very narrow. You completed the audit and provided them with a report and/or opinion. Whoop-dee-do. That is what you were paid to do.

For years, the auditing industry has had a buzzword, "value-added," that goes in and out of vogue. How can we be more value-added? How can we help add value to the client? Sure, you can look for ways to add more value; the best place to start is by understanding the client's challenges and simply asking them. However, you probably already add value in concrete ways and more than you think. In fact, you probably add more value THAN THE CLIENT PERCEIVES. That is your fault!

Perception is reality. If you are a public accountant, it is the client who chooses to pay your bills, it is the client who chooses to retain you, and it is the client who chooses to refer you. If you are an internal auditor, the client is part of your organization! In all cases, it is the client who evaluates you, in one way or another.

Auditors do not always excel in reinforcing to clients the value they deliver. Maybe it is confidence, maybe they were never taught to do so, maybe they do not feel that they have enough time, maybe it's an assumption that it is presumptuous or that the clients don't want it, maybe it is because we have a low perception of our value. Quite possibly, it is because it is not on a checklist! But whatever the reason, we do not do it enough.

So how do you reinforce the value of the service you have provided?

You remind the client of everything you have done for them, including audit-related and nonaudit-related items.

Did you receive a specific schedule or supporting document late, yet you were still able to complete your audit on time? Do you subtly remind the client about that? Do you remind them of all the little examples and all the big obvious ones, too? It is not bragging; it is simply restating the value you provide. Do it formally or informally, whatever it takes for the client to remember all the value you have provided.

Another way to remind clients of your value is to reinforce the compliments THEY GIVE YOU (and your team and other individual team members). A lot of auditors do not take compliments well. They are shy or trying to be humble, or for whatever other reason, they try to dismiss complements quickly.

Acting humble in this way trains your clients not to compliment you in the future. Clients will not feel good about giving compliments. Reverse the situation. How do you want clients to feel when YOU COMPLIMENT THEM? You want them to feel great. You want attention brought their way. You may want others to know about your specific compliment. By acknowledging a compliment, you can actually make the other person feel important. If you are excited about it, if you want them to expand on why they feel that way and you ask follow-up questions, two things may happen:

1. They will want to compliment more. They will search for opportunities to give compliments, because you made them feel good about doing it.
2. They will better remember both delivering the compliment and the specific reason they complimented you.

When a client compliments you or one of your colleagues, ask them follow-up questions if you can. Ask them how what you did made their life easier. Ask them about the specifics so you know how to repeat the actions in the future.

Create Stories

Create long-lasting, memorable stories that your clients will tell others. These can be big or small, peculiar or generic. As long as they are the client's stories, and the clients enjoy telling them to others, it's a way to know you have created memorable client service.

An auditor remembered that a particular client liked to collect souvenir spoons, and when she was on vacation, she found one. It only cost a few dollars, but she bought it and gave it as a gift to the client, who did not even remember telling the auditor he enjoyed collecting them. The client told everyone he could about the gift and story! He told his wife. He told his friends. He told the CFO. He showed everyone in the office. His colleagues came to the auditor and said this was the happiest they had seen that person in weeks! That sounds memorable.

Another auditor created a personalized great customer service survey that he mailed to his annual audit clients quarterly. What was on it? The survey contained nothing special, just the ABCs of serving clients. But the clients liked it; they liked it A LOT. This may sound kind of standard unlike the "spoon" story, but it was not standard to the client. To the client, it was memorable because of its simplicity and what it meant.

Try and learn the names your clients BEFORE you meet them. There are lots of resources out there now to help with this: company Web sites, intranet sites (if you have access), and social sites such as LinkedIn and Facebook. It's a lot easier to find a picture of someone these days. Think to yourself: How would you feel if someone came into your place of business and knew the names of everyone, INCLUDING YOU? Doing this takes time and thoughtfulness. How can this contribute to a positive first impression? You are the auditor ... that is NOT what your clients will expect! If you cannot find a picture, ask the client's Human Resources department whether they have pictures and names and will allow you to have access to them. Tell them why! You will walk into the audit knowing EVERYONE'S name before you are introduced. Kind of cool, a good example of being memorable. Clients pick up on these things: "The auditors took the time to learn our names BEFORE they came here." That, in itself, might be a story the client tells others!

Stories can be general perceptions about you and your team's excellent service, or they can be about specific events. It does not matter. All that matters is that they are the client's positive stories about you!

What stories will your clients tell about you? CREATE THEM.

Turn "Messing Up" into "Stepping Up"

The auditor-client relationship can be very transactional in nature, especially if we allow it to be. But there are still humans on each side of that transaction. We view this relationship as very peculiar in nature, but in most cases, the relationship can be like any vendor/customer relationship. Of course, as in all relationships, there are going to be times where one side messes up, maybe big time.

> Show me someone who has never made a mistake, and I will show you a liar.
>
> —*Harry Redknapp*

Whether you are an internal or external auditor, you must realize that there will be times (hopefully rare) when your team falls short of a client's expectation or just does something blatantly wrong. What do you want to do in these situations? You probably want to feel bad about yourself. You might even be good at that. Well, of course, you want to rectify the situation, too. One key is, if you are working with a team, then you should rectify it as a team. It doesn't matter as much as you might think who actually caused the problem. It is a client problem, so now it is an (entire) audit team problem.

How do you become memorable (in a good way) when something bad happened regarding your client service? You become memorable in how you react to it and how you take responsibility for it.

Here is how you become memorable in a negative way:

- *Play the blame game.* Single out the individual on your team who can be the most easily blamed. Make sure you differentiate between yourself and the others on your team. Break up the team into those who caused the problems and those who did not (which of course includes you!). If the client agrees with any negative thing you might say about your team members, focus on that, because you will have a common frame of reference to expand on as you talk it through. Hopefully, you will feel better by making that other person(s) look worse.
- *Provide excuses.* If you cannot blame anyone else, and the person who is most responsible is obvious—it's YOU—make sure you provide excuses as to why you were not able to meet your responsibility. If you can bring in others as the cause, then do it.
- *Push back on the client.* When the client is mad, argue with them. Try to prove why they are wrong about being mad. Get defensive and either fight back aggressively or avoid them and the conflict. Tell them they

are overreacting. Reach for anything you can to prove them wrong, even if it has nothing to do with the original issue.

■ *Talk about how this happens all the time.* It is common. It is nothing to get riled up about, because it should basically be expected to happen. Their expectations must be too high.

Remember you ARE your company or organization to the client. You are the team and organization representative. They do not want to know that:

■ *They are talking to the wrong person.* Someone else will need to help them.
■ *You are not sure who can help them.* That may be okay. You might not know the exact person who can help, so *assure* them that you are taking responsibility to find out who the best person is. Don't tell them you are not sure; tell them you will find out!

So you messed up and you take care of it. If someone else on your team messed up, should you have to take care of that also? Yes! You must take care of it as far as the client is concerned. Take responsibility. The client, more than anything else, wants to know that someone is taking responsibility for their problem, and they want to know that RIGHT AWAY!

"I will personally see to it that your problem is handled."

Do you know how many people STARVE for these words but never hear them stated explicitly from the vendors they deal with on a day-to-day basis? Valuable time is lost between vendor and client because the client is searching for not just a resolution, but many times, more importantly, someone to take responsibility to ensure a resolution will happen.

Have you ever dealt with a vendor who messed up and took no responsibility? Maybe it was a car dealership, or a cable company, or a phone service provider. You had to call customer service to try and rectify the situation. What many vendors do, in this case, is make you stay on the phone until they are ready to help you. Then invariably, when they cannot help you, they transfer you to someone else or mention that you called the wrong 800 number. Ugh! It is still the same company! Conversely, have you ever called up a vendor with a problem and the person you FIRST talked to took responsibility for getting to the bottom of your problem? That is a breath of fresh air. Maybe they even called you up a day or two later to just make sure everything came out the way you wanted? Awesome.

Now you are on the other side. Actually, it's not very important whether YOU messed up or some else did—what is important is that the TEAM messed up in servicing the client.

The client wants to know that:

- *You want to understand the problem fully and clearly.*

  Listen, listen, and listen some more. When you are done listening, ask follow-up questions to ensure you can listen MORE. You need to understand not just the specifics of the problem but also how it affects them as an organization and personally. Take out a pad of paper, or grab your laptop to take notes! You want to document everything they have to say. Let them SEE you do that. Paraphrase or summarize what they have said to make sure you understand it fully. Use terms that help you clarify, such as:
  - "If I understand you clearly, you are saying ..."
  - "If I am hearing you right ..."
  - "Have I heard everything I need to know about this?"
  - "You are not holding anything back here, are you?"
- *You empathize.*

  If the problem is a big deal to them, shouldn't it be a big deal to you, too? Listen to them not only explain the problem, but how the problem is affecting them. This takes a deep level of listening. You cannot be thinking about your response or your excuses. You must be listening so deeply that you are part of their world. You must hear their perspective.

  Here is a simple example: Someone from the client organization approaches you and tells you how impossible it is for them to get hold of a colleague on your team. There are a few ways you could react to this.

  One of the common reactions is AGREEMENT: "I can never get hold of her either." But that divides the team. Instead, how can you empathize? How can you understand? You do this by understanding the effect that has on your client. Some reactions to consider:
  - "Thank you for telling me that. How has your inability to reach her affected your ability to ... ?"
  - "I am sorry to hear that. I will get in touch with her personally to see that you get an answer to your question."

  Also consider asking the client what the question or problem is and whether you can help. Maybe you cut out the need for the colleague.
- *You take personal responsibility to see their problem is handled.*

  Be careful how you present this. "Handled" is a slightly different word than "fixed" or "solved." If you know you can fix the problem, go ahead and say that, but if you are not sure you can fix it, tell them you will make sure it is *handled*. (Not every problem can be solved.)

If they have any follow-up issues or questions, let them know they can come to you. You are the point person for their problem.

■ *You tell them when you will next get back to them with an update.*

You might not be able to promise a date when the problem will be handled by, but letting them know when you will get back to them next provides an expectation and instills some confidence because you have given them a commitment with a deadline. Consider asking them whether your turnaround time on getting back to them is sufficient. Remember, underpromise and overdeliver!

■ *You thank them!*

Make sure they know how important it was that they spoke up to you. Make sure they know how grateful you are. Make it more personal, if you can: maybe a handwritten thank-you card, maybe a personal note, or a from-the-heart "THANK YOU!" The clients that do not tell you about problems are the clients that will continue to be part of the problems. When they communicate problems, big or small, they have provided you with opportunities.

When you turn a "mess-up" into a major "step up" in the client's eyes, then you become memorable. The client remembers the problem that you (and your team) created...but they also remember your response, and the responsibility you took in solving the problem. They will remember how you handled it, more than how you messed up. They will be even more loyal, because you were truly loyal to them in handling the problem.

Let Clients Guide You

How can you let the client guide your client service? Whether you are an external or internal auditor, the question remains the same. Let's say it a different way: How can you allow yourself to be open enough to allow clients to help you improve your client service? Maybe not just your client service, but everything you do?

First, you have to be willing to be VULNERABLE.

You must be willing to admit that no matter the client and circumstances, your client service can be improved. Why not go to the best source to get tips on how to improve that service: the client. Let the client co-create a vision of really great customer service. Think of this as a high-risk, high-reward opportunity. If you can get the client to co-create the definition of great customer service AND you can deliver that exact level of customer service, then you have done something, something special, with results that you will reap in the area of loyalty.

It may be difficult to think this way with some relationships. The individuals who make up the client organization may not be the most competent in your eyes, and they may not be the easiest people to deal with, but these are still the people that make up your valuable clients. Learn from them.

Second, ask them to provide you their vision of what superior (audit) **service means.**

What are the three, or five, or ten elements of client service that are critical to creating a super-satisfied loyal client? Some *may* include:

- Responsiveness
- Reliability
- Technical expertise
- Listening
- Collaboration

Make sure you have a working definition and questions that should be answered with each of the elements. Some more developed examples include:

- *Responsiveness*. What does being highly responsive mean? What is the client's specific expectation in this area?
- *Collaboration*. What does being highly collaborative mean? How often should we be formally communicating? How do we keep each other up to date on our progress?

Document these elements. The examples above are just that: examples. Create your own elements with your clients. Consider creating customized elements with each of your clients! Opportunities abound when you do this. It involves your clients in defining great service. It also enrolls them in a group effort to deliver great service, leading to a more efficient audit.

Take *responsiveness*, for example. The answers to these questions will help you to know how responsive you need to be, but they may also enable you to actually be LESS responsive than you have been (based on assumptions made about the client). Do they need all questions answered immediately? If something is very critical, what is a good response time? Both of you will define that FOR BOTH PARTIES!

Now let's look at *collaboration*. This element does not just mean how you continuously "collaborate" with them, but also it focuses attention on how well they collaborate with you.

Both parties should participate in the process of creating these elements. Both parties contribute by elaborating on what is important to them within the elements. And both parties win.

Third, you must continually measure your progress.

Don't just define the critical elements with the client and then shove them in some drawer. Revisit them often with your team and the client.

Consider getting your team to document specific examples of how you lived up to these expectations developed by the client. Categorize your examples based on the elements the client co-created with you.

Earlier in this chapter, we discussed how reminding clients of the value (all of it) you provide is important. This "element tracking process" can provide you with a formal method of doing just that! The key here is the client co-created the measurement criteria!

Track your progress. Make it part of your evaluations completed by the client. Let them tell you how you excelled in the elements by providing examples that you did not even remember or document!

Be Yourself

Do you want to be memorable to clients? Be yourself. That is right ... be yourself *more*. What are the characteristics and typical actions you make outside of work that people do not always see inside your office walls and your client's office walls?

Many people act different at work than they do at home and around friends—for good reason, in some cases! But reflect on the positive things you do in your personal life, the things you enjoy doing and feel natural doing. Which of those translate into providing memorable client service?

Do you like to send birthday cards or holiday cards to friends? Why not do it to clients? Even a client you may never see again?

Do you enjoy giving small gifts to people?

Do you have similar hobbies to a client?

Did you just read a book that you feel an individual at the client organization might enjoy?

When the client can see (1) more of who you really are, and (2) that you are trying to share that with them in personal ways that HELP them, chances are they will want to do the same thing for you. They will see you less as an auditor and more as a person who is looking for personal ways to help them. Be yourself! Also, don't forget to encourage others on your team to be themselves more, as well.

One Client at a Time

Only your clients can tell you whether you are memorable—not you, not your team. The clients are the evaluators. You must figure out whether they see you as memorable. You need to go to the source and get the score from them.

One would expect that the more "memorable" your team is in many of the areas we discussed, the more likely you are to get referrals, right?

So ask questions. "Will you refer us?" is a very close-ended question that does not provide you any information. The better questions might be:

- WHY (specifically) will you refer us?
- HOW (specifically) will you refer us?

These questions rock, because they serve as a referendum on your MEMORABLE customer service. If you are an external auditor, it's a referral for another audit client. If you are an internal auditor, it's a referral to others inside your organization for YOUR MEMORABLE SERVICE!

Leadership Summary

How do "auditors" provide memorable client service?

- Continually search for opportunities to create "stories."
- Turn inevitable "mess-ups" into opportunities to demonstrate how you can "step up" in the client's eyes.
- Let clients formally show you, by co-creating the most important elements of client service, and then measuring your progress using those criteria.
- Be yourself.
- Ask the client.

How do you become memorable? You let CLIENTS SHOW YOU!

PART VI

Teambuilding and Reflection Skills

CHAPTER 21

Prepare to Be Fired

"I know I should have delegated this, but it was faster for me to get it
  done myself."
"I wanted to take more vacation time, but I have too much work to get
  done."
"I don't have time to explain this."
"I am the only one who can do this."
"If it wasn't for me, there is no way this would get finished."

You have probably heard comments similar to this. You may have *made*
comments similar to this.

These types of comments (and the attitude that comes with them)
present a huge opportunity. The opportunity is for you to start leading
more, plain and simple, by empowering those around you. You need to
make those around you so important and so skilled that they do not need
you to do what they and you (as a team) are currently doing. You become
unnecessary. You become obsolete. You get yourself fired, because you are
not needed anymore.

The main ingredient in stardom is the rest of the team.
                                                        —*John Wooden*

You want to be fired from what you are currently doing, so you can
move on to new things, new responsibilities, a promotion, other tasks that
you want to do, and opportunities in which you can best use your strengths
to help your organization!

Take another look at the five quotes above. What is the first word in four
of the five sentences? "I." The fifth one has "me." How do you value your
skills within your organization? If your value is limited simply by your ability
to get YOUR tasks done, that is fine, but you must realize that your potential

will be limited—by YOU. That is great if you want to own your very own one-person audit shop, or you desire to have a position somewhere that requires little interaction with anyone else on the planet.

Prepare to Be Fired from the Very Beginning: Leadership Transition

Let's say you are a manager and you are introducing the senior auditor to the client for the first time.

"Hi, this is Suzy. She is going to be the acting senior on this job, and one day she will be a manager. That day will probably be happening pretty soon with the way her career is going."

What does that type of introduction do?

- It affirms your belief in your colleague.
- It sets the tone that you see your colleague as an integral part of your team, and that you want the client to see that also.
- It provides an expectation to the client about the senior's ability and role, and his or her FUTURE ROLE. The future role aspect is very important. Many auditors have a hard time with "leadership transition" on projects. They might try and include the protégés in meetings with the client, but unless the client EXPECTS the leadership transition, unless the client has been formally prepped for it, it may seem awkward or quickly forced. The client sometimes gets fixated in seeing that employee as a senior unless you give them a "preview" of the next phase of the employee's career.

How important are sterling introductions to you? Do you believe they can help with first impressions? Do you believe they can help with leadership transition?

If you are a staff auditor who will be working with an intern, if you are a manager working with a senior, or if you are an executive working with a manager, start from the very beginning of your relationship with a vision of how you will help them MOVE UP within the organization. Share that vision not only with audit clients, but also with them.

Be explicit with your mentee about how you will help them move up. Get buy-in from them. Get ideas from them. Have them help you co-create the process. Do it early. Do it right away. Some questions to consider:

"One of my goals is to ensure you move up as fast as you can in this organization. How are we doing?"
"I was looking at my personal goals for the upcoming year, and one of them is centered on supporting you. Could you spend some time in

thinking about how I can support you better? Specific ideas would be very welcomed."

"How often should you and I meet so that we can ensure your skills are progressing at the rate you want?" (or "at the fastest rate possible?")

"Based on the typical progression of someone your level, you are set to be promoted to (level) by (date). How do you feel you are doing? How am I doing in helping?"

"Talk to me about how you feel about proceeding to the next level in our organization. What are the things that excite you about that?"

"How can I empower you to take on more responsibilities? Are there ways I might be stifling your growth and ability to take on more responsibilities?"

"I can see you taking over my position very soon, and probably doing a better job at it. Do you see this? Do you want this? How do we, together, get you there? What are some of the unique abilities you will bring to that new position? What are the activities that you truly enjoy doing and how do they keep your momentum going? Are there any skills you would like to work on related to that?"

"What are the responsibilities that you would like to have that you do not have right now? Talk to me about how taking those new responsibilities can help the team, the company, and your growth."

"How do we plan the leadership transition on that audit? I do not believe it is ever too early for us to start thinking about that."

Un-Empowering Statements and Questions

Beware of these phrases:

"Can we take a step back for a second."—Potential translation: You are not seeing the bigger picture here. I need to tell you to step back and rethink this from a better perspective.

"Repeat back to me what I just said."—Potential translation: I am not sure you know what you are doing, so I need to handhold you tightly to ensure you know exactly what I just told you to do and how I told you to do it.

"I do not think you understand the big picture here."—Potential translation: You are not very bright.

Not only do these types of questions demonstrate your belief in your colleagues and reports, but they also set the stage for their development. They set the stage for leadership transition.

They are also mentoring questions! Think about how you would feel if someone asked you questions like this. Would it inspire you? Would it challenge you to take a look at your job, responsibilities, and career? Would it help you focus on where you want to go next within the company? You can ask these types of questions of someone with whom you have just started working, too. How would you feel if, within your first few weeks, one of your bosses or colleagues asked you similar questions to these? Pumped?

You need to answer the questions. They will help you figure out the bigger questions: Where are you going as a team? And where are the individuals who make up the team going? By asking questions like those above, you'll find out, and you'll help get them there.

Born to Be Skeptical

What happens when I excel in "transition leadership," but then that same person who was being prepared to step in picks up and leaves our organization?

This is bound to happen. In our profession, it is certain to happen. But how does that change your mentoring and leading of other people? It is not a waste. What you have done is (1) helped develop that other person, and (2) sharpened your own leadership transition skills. The development and improvement of your leadership transition process will only lead to good things in your career.

Even if they leave, most of them will not forget you. You have helped them, so you have strengthened your social capital!

Also, as you have probably heard, leadership succession and succession planning in the accounting (and auditing) industry is going to be a really big deal in the near and far future, given the lopsided bell-shaped curve of the workforce. Baby Boomers are going to be retiring in droves soon (even after many delay retirement), leaving a major need for succession of leadership at audit shops all around the country, and the small Gen X and larger (but younger) Gen Y workforces are going to need to pick up the slack. Transition leadership prepares you for leadership succession.

Add More Responsibilities

When is the best time to challenge your staff and colleagues to push themselves to take on more responsibility?

- *When they have just hit a home run!*

    If someone has just finished a project and did a great job, if someone just received a great review, then they are probably ready to take a further step. In cases like this, consider giving them at least one additional responsibility, even if it is one that does not take up much time, above their "pay grade." Why? It reinforces their achievement. It reinforces their growth. They climbed a step in their career, so show them the next step (upward), even if it is a small one.

- *When they ask for it.*

    If someone asks for new responsibilities, then by all means, if they are ready, give the responsibilities to them. If they seem bored with their work, the opportunity for more responsibility might be there. Make sure you are always listening to their engagement levels. There may be other reasons why they are not fully engaged in their job, but one reason might be the lack of challenges.

- *Before they MUST add them.*

    Some organizations have formal development programs that provide milestones for employees to hit and new responsibilities to be delegated. Others do not. In either case, some of this development must be done at an individual level. Also, if there is a rigid development plan, see if you cannot challenge it, when your employees and colleagues are ready to take on additional responsibility ahead of the times that some "guidelines and policies" say they should.

They See, They Do

Some of the considerations and tips mentioned in this book appear to be related to personal skills. They may be. But they are also part of your leadership and mentoring skills, whether that is obvious or not.

People are impressionable—some more, and some less, but we are all impressionable to some degree. All of these skills may appear "personal" on the surface, but they are viewable to others. If you want to be fired, you need to be cognizant of your influence on others, including how your own (personal) skills rub off on them.

Your personal time management skills—others see those every day. Do you continually miss meetings or have to reschedule them? That is contagious.

More on Mentoring

In the last decade many companies have taken mentoring more seriously, with the implementation of more formal programs. Some have done well, others have struggled. What are some things to consider at your organization and in your personal mentoring relationships?

- *Mentoring starts at the top.*

    If your company takes the mentoring of its employees seriously, then shouldn't executive leadership be involved? Why shouldn't your CEO, CAO, or Managing Partner be a mentor also?

    Don't be shy in selecting your mentor, even if it is done informally. Are you just a lowly staff person (who is about to take your leadership skills to a new level)? Maybe you need a very good mentor. Why not aim high, and do not worry about what level the mentor is?

- *Mentors need to be CHOSEN, not assigned.*

    One of the key success factors in a mentoring relationship is just that—the RELATIONSHIP. If it is forced, it has little chance of flourishing. Even if you have a formal mentor who was assigned to you, there is no reason why you should not look for someone else if the relationship is awkward. Many companies are realizing this and allowing the mentees to have more input in the relationship choice.

- *If mentoring matters, measure it and reward for it.*

    If it really matters, it should be part of your employees' job responsibilities, and/or it should be part of their evaluation, it should be encouraged by your organization's core leadership, and linked to promotions, benefits, and pay.

    Be a rebel. If your organization does not measure the benefit of mentoring relationships, do it yourself. Get feedback. Make it part of informal (or formal) evaluations.

- *Mentors need mentors, too.*

    Don't ever feel like you are too "high" on the totem pole to need a mentor. You can learn a lot from being a mentee. You can learn a lot about developing better mentoring skills by being a mentee.

Your e-mail management skills—others see those every day, maybe many times a day! Do you have 972 e-mails stuck in your inbox right now, some needing a reply? How responsive can you be perceived to be in this scenario? That is contagious, too.

If you do not solicit feedback from your colleagues very often, they may not feel comfortable soliciting it from you.

If you do not know your teammates very well, chances are they will not get to know you well.

If you do not start out your day in a positive state of mind, others might pick up the same habit.

If you do not listen well ... If you do not provide your full attention and fully focus on them when they are talking ... If you are multitasking while they are talking ... If you are thinking about other things, stressing about other things when they are talking ... then there is much more of a chance that they will do the same thing. It is all contagious.

Listening Skills

You have been told many times by many different people how important listening is, so let's talk about it one more time! Do you:

- Exude enthusiasm for the opportunity to listen to others?
- Ask questions to not only ensure you understand what they are saying, but also their personal perspective? Can you hear "how" they are talking so that you can pick up limiting beliefs or frustrations?
- Block out all possible interruptions when listening to others?
- Clear your mind when listening to others? Do you clear it of stereotypes, assumptions, and preconceived notions about the other person or what they might say? If you feel like you already know what they are going to say, you will have a hard time *listening* to what they will say, and your assumption can very well be wrong!
- Project a position of neutrality? If you want to listen and assess well, you need to be neutral when you are gathering information (listening). The assessments, opinions, conclusions can come later, but only after you have *listened* to the other person as much as you can.
- Remember what the other person is saying? If it goes in one ear and out the other, how focused are you?
- Ask to get feedback from others on your listening skills?

Have you ever walked into an executive's office and could barely get past their door because papers were piled everywhere and books and folders were thrown all over the floor? Is that wrong? Not necessarily, but what do you think that type of example sets for the others in the organization? Is that someone you want to emulate regarding personal organization?

Once again, this touches on mentoring. Isn't a "mentor," whether the person is set up in a formal mentoring program or an informal mentor, someone you want to emulate?

Who is emulating you? (Probably more people than you think.)

Team Accountability

What does the word *accountability* mean? Accountability is taking responsibility for results. It is being answerable for results. Team accountability is the ENTIRE team taking responsibility for the results of the team, in comparison to their objectives and goals.

What would happen if you were to be gone for a long time, starting TOMORROW? Ask yourself this question. Ask your team this question. Is there one person on your team who is the "enforcer," who ensures that everything gets done and people do what they are told to do no matter what? What happens if that person is not present? How can you be fired if you are irreplaceable? How can the team go on without you, if you are the only person holding others accountable for their actions and the results?

What is one of the best ways to create team accountability?

ASK THE TEAM how that should work. Maybe go further and ask them what is important to the TEAM. Include items such as:

- Meeting milestones
- Being prepared for meetings—What happens if we aren't? What happens if one person is not prepared?
- Communicating mishaps right away
- Sharing important information with other team members

You can create other items. You and your teams can create items that are personalized to the specific team, to the individuals on the team, and even to the audit and/or client.

However, before you do that, you must first ensure that the team knows where it is going! Does everyone know what our specifically defined achievements will be? It's not as simple as "to get the audit completed." When does it need to be done? What are the key milestones that allow us to get the ENTIRE audit completed on time? What does "done" mean? What are other goals we have? What tasks and projects have been delegated? Are their individual growth or skill development goals? Why not share those with EVERYONE (so the team can be accountable for those "individual" goals)?

Team accountability also demands team buy-in. What is the commitment of the individuals to the team's future achievements? What is the commitment of the individual team players to the other individual team player's responsibilities? That is why co-creation of the team's accountability methods can be a powerful exercise. If they co-create accountability aspects, the opportunity for buy-in from all individuals increases dramatically.

More Tips for Delegating Tasks and Projects

- *Determine the best delegation style.* Here are two general styles to consider:

  Directive style—Tell them exactly what to do. Be specific. This style usually works well with someone who lacks the technical skill and/or confidence to get it done without step-by-step instruction. Focus on detailed steps.

  Delegating style—Tell them what you need, but be less specific about the details. They will figure that out. They have the acumen, they have the experience, and they have the know-how necessary to get through the details. They just need to know what you want. Focus on objectives.

- *Visualize the end product and the outcome.* Make sure they know what that looks like, also. What is the specific final product? Even if you must use a very directive style, what is required (the end product) is much more important than the "task" or "process" part of delegating.

- *Fit what they are doing into the big picture.* Why is it important? Tell them how you will use what they are going to deliver. (This also, once again, reminds them of the importance.)

- *Communicate belief.* Tell them exactly why you are sure they can get it done and what resources they have available to them.

- *Co-create expectations.* You need to know when it is going to get done. You may even know when you MUST have it done. That does not stop you from getting some input from them. "I'll need to start with this next step by November 10, so when can I expect

(continued)

(*continued*)

   you to get this to me?" Challenge them to underpromise to you on
   the deadline.
- *Create an accountability expectation.* Do you need to follow up
  midway? Consider asking them when you should follow-up on their
  progress. If you agree to a specific follow-up time, don't let them
  down!
- *Review the delegation/achievement after it is done.* You believed in
  them before the delegation, they came through. Now make note
  of that. If the project or task was a big deal, consider making a big
  deal of their achievement. Ask them why they delivered on time.
  Do they feel good about it? What did you do to help? What could
  you have done better?

Team Chemistry

Surround yourself with COMPLEMENTARY people, or uncover complementary strengths in those around you.

What does that mean? Notice the strengths in others that you do not
have. Point them out. Be happy with them being the expert above you
in certain areas. If you are a level-one employee, this is easy, but it takes
confidence to do this when you are the boss. Everyone has weaknesses. See
if you cannot use your weaknesses to your ADVANTAGE by searching for
others on your team who do not share them. You cannot always choose the
people with whom you work, but you can choose to uncover the strengths
of those around you and use them. Find a strength in another person that
is a weakness in you!

Are you always searching for the strengths of your colleagues? For those
on your specific teams or those whom you work with a lot, ask them what
they perceive to be their strengths.

The traditional concept of delegating, in which you realize a task needs
to get finished soon and THEN look for delegation opportunities, is overrated. That is task delegation. There is nothing wrong with doing that, and
it can save you some time and make your team more efficient in the short
term. But if you want to "be fired" from your current responsibilities and
make *your organization* more efficient and effective in the long run, focus
on the delegation of responsibilities and process ownership by proactively
empowering others.

The best coaches in any team sport do an inventory of their players'
talents and strengths first. Only THEN do they design the schemes and

plays to call during games, to use those strengths. Have you ever, while planning an audit, considered the strengths of those involved, regardless of their level? Have you ever caught yourself struggling over a particular task, maybe writing a memo, and delegated it to someone else—not because you did not have time, but because you thought they could do a better job with it?

If you continuously seek to uncover the strengths of others, then you empower them and you empower the team, and suddenly, once again, you become less needed.

The "Open Door" Leader

As we discussed in Chapter 11, some auditors take an open-door policy too literally. They have their door physically open all day, or they are accessible to anyone who comes close to their cube. This can be counterproductive, because it "opens" you to continuous interruptions. It also reinforces sporadic interruptions from others, which is counterproductive to THEIR productivity.

So how do you become more open to your colleagues without having to physically have your door open all day?

If you want to be fired, you will need to have powerful collaborative relationships with your key colleagues. You must intentionally "design" the relationship.

People positively care more about having ACCESS to you than they care about having small interruption time with you. In fact, many times, you can probably remember being interrupted by someone and as you are finishing up with the first interruption (and are transitioning to the next thing you need to do, or worse, spending time trying to remember what you were doing), you notice that the person is hesitating to leave your area, and is trying to think of other questions he or she can ask you! Why is that? It is because that person is not sure when you will have time for him or her again. It is so sporadic that the person feels the urge to ask you as many questions as possible, because the person HAS YOUR ATTENTION NOW. What ensues? Your people tug at you when they can, they grab you in the hall when they see you, and they interrupt you if it is possible. They are just trying to get their jobs done. If your work life sounds a lot like this, then it is because both parties have come to expect it. It is the norm. The relationship has been "designed" to work this way.

How do you challenge the norm? You replace sporadic communication with consistent communication. The people with whom you work on a regular basis need to have consistent, reliable, scheduled communication with you. When? How often? You decide. Both parties need to decide together. Both parties contribute to formally "design" the relationship by answering such questions and revisiting them going forward. You will find yourself spending longer doses of time together, but overall it will be less time, because you will both have confidence in having access to each other, access that allows you to have full focus on helping each other!

Dave Crenshaw, in his book *The Myth of Multitasking*, says, "When we give people segmented attention, piecemeal time, switching back and forth, the switching cost is higher than just the time involved. We end up damaging relationships."

I wonder if there is a positive spin here too. If you are able to set aside consistently predictable time with your key colleagues so that you both can be PRESENT and attentive to each other, how does that ENHANCE your relationships? They will not expect it. They might not even be comfortable with it at first. You explain it. YOU LEAD IT.

Teach Your Teams to Seek Complaints

How many people do you work with or come across every day that complain, gripe, or whine constantly?

When you hear this often from those on YOUR teams, consider what you can do:

- Jump on board the complaint bandwagon
- Ignore it
- Determine the root of the complaints and work through them

You have probably already formed an opinion about which of these three options is the most preferable. It's probably not the first option; maybe it is a combination of the second and third, depending on the situation.

If you want to be fired, **you must install a process in your teams for dealing with internal complaints** and excuses. Complaints and excuses are not wrong; they are what they are. The key is uncovering the root of the problems so that EVERYONE, including those who make them, can be part of the solution. Whether that is creating the solution, implementing it, or holding people accountable for maintaining it, they all need to be aware of the process. Ask your team how you (the team) should deal with internal complaints? Have we created an open environment where people are comfortable in bringing up complaints? Invite complaints and create an environment where they are sought. It builds trust within your team.

Ponder Your Future Often

You cannot graduate from what you are doing and your responsibilities if you do not plan for it. It is easy to allow the daily things that pull at you to take up ALL your time.

In the December 29, 2008, issue of *Time*, then-President-elect Barack Obama was asked about advice he had received from past presidents just before he took office. He said, "I can tell you that all of them said it is important to carve out time to think and not spend your entire day reactive. Because there is always a crisis coming at you, there's always a meeting you could be doing, there's always a press conference or a group of supporters that you could be responding to. And so I think maintaining that kind of discipline is important."

We might not have many press conferences to attend, or groups of supporters to talk to, but it is eerie how much the rest of what he said holds true for our daily lives as auditors.

If you want to be fired, you will need to carve out time to start thinking about your future and the futures of those around you. This allows you to graduate from what you are currently doing and it also allows you to create what you want to be doing.

Your Professional Long-Term Goals

When setting long-term goals for your career:

- *Review what you stand for.*

  Review your draft mission statement, if you have one (see Chapter 1), and your values. When creating goals, ask yourself how they help you in your mission. What does achieving your long-term goals mean to you? How will you feel once you have completed them?
- *Get feedback from others around you.*

  Where do the other leaders of your organization see you going? What goals can you create that help you get there (if you share their vision)? What are the organization's goals? If you have a mentor, run them by her or him. If you have a mentee, do the same. (Sounds nontraditional, but you might be surprised about their feedback and the effect it might have on them.)
- *Consider how others contribute to your goals.*

  How will others contribute to you reaching your goals? KEEP OTHERS (continuously) AWARE OF THEM. This is a big issue, and

(continued)

(continued)

an often-overlooked strategy. Do you want to be "fired" from what you are doing right now? You need to enroll other leaders in your goals so (1) they are complementary to the organization's goals and vision, and (2) they can help you with accountability. The more you develop into a leader, the more help you will need from others!

- *Document your goals!*

  Try to make them specific, short (if you cannot remember it, it is probably too long), reasonable (don't overcommit!), measurable, time-sensitive, and inspiring.

  By June, I will celebrate passing the CPA exam.

  On January 1, 20XX, I will be an audit senior manager. (I plan to thank my staff for all their contributions that will make that possible.)

  By the end of the fiscal year, we will complete all the IT audits identified. (We have already planned the party we will hold upon completing these.)

  I will retire by the time I am 60, with $_____ saved.

- *Set aside time for continuous reflection.*

  Ask yourself: How am I doing? What is working and what is not? WHY? Do I need to tweak my goals? Are the milestones clear? Where am I right now, versus where I thought I would be?

Are long-term goals overrated in today's fast-paced business world? Maybe, maybe not. Most leaders will tell you they are essential, but YOU must CHOOSE to develop them, and you must practice the discipline to achieve them. It is pretty easy not to create them and not to achieve them!

If you feel that long-term goals are worthless because you do not have TIME to create them, monitor them, or achieve them, or if you feel like long-term goals are not as important as short-term goals because of the speed at which a person's career changes, fair enough.

If long-term goals have not worked for you in the past, try something different. "Connect your dots." Steve Jobs used this term in a 2005 commencement speech when describing his life to the graduating students of Stanford; the speech is available on YouTube.com if you want to check it out. What does "connecting your dots" mean? Spend some time reflecting on your history. What were the big events that led you to where you are right now in your career? What were the big decisions? What were your big achievements? In this way, you can uncover the goals that you achieved in the past, even if you did not set them, that have placed you exactly where you are today. Now, after reviewing your past successes, you might be able to look at your future more easily.

The simplest way to differentiate between short- and long-term goals is by time. The long-term goal, obviously, takes longer to achieve than the short-term goal. Strong long-term goals allow you to "realize" something, too, because achieving them brings you to a new place in your life.

You may realize, in reflecting on your goals, that you already have some long-term goals, you just have not formalized them. The power of documenting goals is that it formalizes them. You can review them more often, memorize them, share them, and then, when you achieve them … celebrate them!

Leadership Summary

Prepare to "Be Fired" from your current role and responsibilities:

- Intentionally plan "leadership transition" with your teams.
- Proactively add new responsibilities to those around you *when they are most ready for them*. That empowers.
- Strengthen the teams you are part of by introducing accountability, improving team chemistry, having a predictably open door, and teaching them to "seek" problems.
- Reflect on and plan your future and the futures of those around you consistently.

CHAPTER 22

Now Where Are You Going?

While working with accountants, I have seen many of them create inspiring goals for themselves; many of the goals were specific and measurable. When they reached their goals it was easy to know—and it was usually time to celebrate.

As you are reading this book, you may choose to create some goals for yourself. You may choose to start acting in new ways, and you may choose to challenge yourself to become a better leader. (We provide you a template of how you might plan your approach on the last page of this chapter.)

Success Is a Mind-Set, Not a Finish Line

Keep in mind, though, while achieving goals and changing behaviors might be measurable, success is NOT measurable. Success is not reaching goals or getting rewarded or recognized. Success is a state of mind. It is determined by you and only you. Winning an award for employee of the year might mean success for one person, and it might not for another. It is your internal state of mind, how YOU FEEL about that award, that matters. Only you control that because, well, only you control your mind! Only you can determine what being successful means, because only you can feel it.

A colleague comes up to you and congratulates you on doing a great job on a specific project or audit. Does that mean you have succeeded? No, it means that you have a moment to decide whether you want to feel you are successful, in that moment.

Have you ever experienced a day filled with unfinished projects, feelings of frustration and stress, yet something happened at the end of the day that had you feeling great? Maybe you finally figured out how to fix the kitchen sink. Maybe you received a message from a long-lost friend. Maybe someone in your family had some great news to share with you. Maybe a client or colleague reached out to you and told you what a great job you did on the last audit. If the feelings you had about that late-day event were heartfelt enough, they probably washed away all the frustration of your day. The stressful open projects were still there for you at work, they just did not pull at you as much, because those other feelings you gained from the later "success" trumped them. You have probably heard the phrase "success breeds success." Maybe (strong) feelings of success also trump feelings of not feeling successful?

The fact of the matter is you can be successful RIGHT NOW. You only have to feel successful. You do not need to be famous, you do not need to be rich, you do not need anyone else to tell you how successful you are, and you do not need anyone else to confirm your success. If you are always looking for confirmation from outside forces and people, then you are bound to be let down, because outsiders will never be able to control your success. Only you can feel it.

Have you ever felt good in a moment of perceived failure, maybe when you came up short in reaching a specific goal? Even if you didn't feel good at that exact moment, maybe you felt good later, when you reflected on it? You did your best, you learned a lot about yourself, and you pushed yourself hard. You just did not reach your goal. Some people can feel better about themselves when they come up short in reaching their goals than others do when they blow right past them. Why is that? It's because of the choice to feel successful. That is success. It is you choosing to feel good about your accomplishments, but it's also about you feeling good about who you are, who you are TODAY, right now.

Some people may have deep-rooted issues in giving themselves permission to feel successful. They are always looking for more, comparing themselves to others, feeling inferior, and feeling as though they do not measure up to their image of what success should "look like." They might not ever be successful in their own minds, because what they see in themselves right now is not what their picture of success looks like. Success does not look like anything. Success feels like something, and it must be a choice. Why might one person feel successful in receiving an award, while another will not? It's because it is their choice.

Ralph Waldo Emerson wrote a "success poem," as follows:

What Is Success?

To laugh often and much;

To win the respect of intelligent people and the affection of children;

To earn the appreciation of honest critics and endure the betrayal of false friends;

To appreciate beauty;

To find the best in others;

To leave the world a bit better, whether by a healthy child, a garden patch, or a redeemed social condition;

To know even one life has breathed easier because you have lived;

This is to have succeeded.

That poem is great. In it, Emerson tells us exactly the actions and realizations he needed to feel successful. His points are well written and may be inspirational, but that is just his take. We all want to feel successful, but we all, individually, must define what will get us there, now and in the future. Our definitions will all be different, and we will not always know the exact path.

If you want to know whether someone else is successful, don't analyze their accomplishments and try and make the call yourself. *Ask them* whether they are successful. Only they know, because only they know whether they feel success. That probably sounds weird, but it reinforces the point. If you really want to improve your awareness about others and your relationships at the same time, you will need to get personal with people and have a desire to uncover and understand their feelings, just as you must do the same thing with YOURSELF.

If you read this book in an effort to help make you more successful, then you may be disappointed. Although the phrases *success* and *critical success factors* have been tossed around throughout the chapters, the only one who can gauge and feel success is you. Do you choose to be successful? If so, maybe the first step is to answer this question: Do you choose to see yourself, right now, as successful? It is a choice—your choice. Only you make it. ARE YOU SUCCESSFUL? Do you give yourself permission, right now, to feel success based on who you are right now and where you are in your life? Can you see that everything that has happened in your life, all the difficult events, all the challenges, all the achievements, all the failures, the bad times, the good times ... these have served as a means by which you have come to the place and the person you are today.

This book was created to provide you with ideas to reflect on, and in doing so, we hope you have come to realize the importance of being more reflective about what you do. We hope you have also come to realize the importance of being more intentional about what you do.

Being self-reflective and intentional is a big struggle for many auditors, who are so process-driven and results-driven that they sometimes forget to reflect on how they can make real improvements in their life and how they can be truly intentional about their growth. Remember, it's very difficult to be reflective when you are busy. It is difficult to improve your leadership skills when you have 15 minutes left to get a report finished before a deadline. If this book provided you with one general thing to think about,

I hope that it helped you turn on your reflective side about your leadership and professional skills and how you want to "lead" your own life, both inside and outside of your office walls.

Grand, tear-dropping growth and self-actualization almost never comes from a training class, conference, book, or article. It comes from uncovering who you are and letting that shine out brightly to the world. Only you can do that. Only you can be self-aware.

Awareness Unlocks Who You Are

> Awareness is the greatest agent of change.
>
> —*Eckhart Tolle*

Have you ever been in a dream and then realized you were in the dream while you were still in it? Maybe it was a dream that involved frustration, such as trying to walk up a steep hill and continually falling down. Maybe you were trying to run somewhere, maybe run away from something or someone, but you were stuck in slow-motion. When you were dreaming, you were grinding it out, but you were unaware of your predicament. You were unaware of why you were not running as fast as you wanted or why you were falling down.

You were unable to change what was happening, until YOU REALIZED it was a dream. You probably did not start to run fast once you realized it was a dream. Upon your awareness, you realized YOU DID NOT HAVE TO RUN FASTER OR STOP FROM FALLING DOWN because you realized the simple truth: You were not stuck, and you were not falling down. It was all changed by your AWARENESS. The frustration suddenly went away.

When you are dreaming, you are thinking, and for that short time, that becomes your reality. Once you know you are dreaming, you become aware that the dream is not real, and you realize your true reality.

Think about life the same way. You are living day to day, but how much are you reflecting on what you are doing? All the ideas presented in this book that you WANT TO MAKE HAPPEN, along with all the ideas YOU CREATED while reading this book ... they required you to not just read, but to read while thinking about yourself. You had to be reflective about what you were currently doing, what you want, and what you choose to do about that in the future.

There is a saying in sports: "If you are not getting better, you are getting worse." If you are not getting better at understanding yourself, there is no way you can uncover who you are and how you can make leadership strides.

What Are the Leadership Skills You Uncovered and Want to Develop?

If you want to *be* more successful, you must become *aware* of what makes you *feel* successful.

　　You must be aware of what you are currently doing.

　　You must be aware of what you want to change.

　　You must be aware of what you will do to change.

　　If you choose to review this book a second time, reread certain parts of it, or look at parts you chose to highlight, take note of the chapters or sections that really hit home with you. They probably meant something, because you realized you already do some of these things, or you imagined how you might make improvements, and that made you feel good about yourself EVEN BEFORE YOU implemented any changes or made any improvements.

> It is kind of ironic that we can feel good about making changes to our lives even before we make them, but it's true.
>
> 　　Ben Stiller, playing Derek Zoolander in the comedy *Zoolander*, made light of this point when he said, "I have deeper thoughts on my mind. The other day, I was thinking about volunteering to help teach underprivileged children to learn how to read. And just thinking about it was the most rewarding experience I've ever had."

　　In many ways, we attract the leadership skills we want to have, because those are the skills we FEEL GOOD (and feel successful) by demonstrating. **We may already have these skills** to some degree; they are just buried deep down because we struggle to be more self-aware on a daily basis, allowing the world to dictate what we do and become versus being fully aware of what is important to us and what is already inside us.

　　Let's review some of the skills and ideas presented in this book … in the form of questions. Answer them, and continue to uncover what is important to you and where you have big potential to grow, achieve, and *feel* successful. Then turn to page 225 and, if you CHOOSE, use the "Your Plan" template presented to create a plan for yourself by answering the questions provided.

Chapter 1—Where Are You Going?

- What are the most important roles you serve in your life?
- What do you systematically do to add value to those roles?

- What are your core values?
- What types of behaviors do you demonstrate in living your values?
- Who knows your values?
- How can defining your mission, even if it is going to change, provide you with clarity, motivation, and energy? How can that help you find purpose in your vocation?

Chapter 2—Selling Number One

- How do you "sell yourself" every day?
- What are the things you do consistently that represent your personal brand?
- How do you introduce yourself? How do you introduce what you do?
- How does uncovering your brand and formally documenting it give you confidence when you practice the principles that make it up consistently?

Chapter 3—Feedback Equals Money

- How important is feedback to you?
- What sources of feedback do you use?
- How can obtaining feedback from others open the door to providing it to those same people?
- Are you continuously evaluating your colleagues' performance?
- How do you reinforce the good things your colleagues do with consistent feedback?
- How do you provide very specific feedback that people can understand and use?
- How do you show others that the feedback they have provided is important? How do you follow up with them LATER to show them how their feedback made a difference in your development, the team's development, and improvements to the organization?
- How can soliciting feedback from others make them feel important?
- How can you make feedback contagious at your organization?

Chapter 4—The Audit Cheerleader

- How do you build belief among your team members?
- How can you see conflict as an opportunity for growth?
- How do you handle conflict? How do you depersonalize conflict?
- How do you create a "home-field" advantage for your teams? How do you continuously build others up?

- Have you identified reusable sources of motivation and inspiration?
- How do you surround yourself with positive influences?
- How can being more appreciative about what you already have help you be more productive in the future?
- How can you demonstrate strong leadership skills (and humility) with your "enemies"?

Chapter 5—Your Social Capital

- How do you inventory the professional relationships you already have?
- Who is in your circle of trust? Who should be?
- How do you strengthen your own social capital by strengthening others?

Chapter 6—The First Step in Networking

- How can you see your CURRENT professional relationships as potential 20-year relationships?
- How can you challenge your mindset when networking so that your biggest goal is to find others you can assist?
- How can you improve your networking skills so that you are searching for and building relationships?

Chapter 7—The Most Important Word to an Auditor

- How can you make long-term and daily improvements to what you are doing by asking WHY more often?
- How can you teach others to ask "why" more and to search for *why* answers?

Chapter 8—The Problem with To-Do Lists

- How do you turn ambiguous To-Do items into specific action steps?
- How do you reconcile your To-Do lists and your new action lists with your overall goals? When do you do that? How often?

Chapter 9—The Power of Time-Blocking

- How can you be more realistic in scheduling your activities by using buffers?
- How do you use time-blocking to say "no" more often?
- How can you use time-blocking to block distractions and interruptions?
- How do you protect the time you need to do the things you want to get done?

Chapter 10—The Power of Routines

- What healthy routines are you already doing?
- In which areas of your life would the creation of healthy habits and routines help you fulfill the most important roles you serve? What are some routines that can be created, based on things you are already doing, that might make you more efficient?
- What kinds of powerful names can you give to routines that involve your teams, your colleagues at work, your friends outside of work, or your family?
- How can you help to create group accountability for group routines to ensure they happen?

Chapter 11—Do You Train Your People to Interrupt You?

- How do you become intentionally accessible during certain times, so that you can be interrupted less often?
- How do you empower others so that they do not NEED to interrupt you?

Chapter 12—Do You Have Commitment Issues?

- How do you keep track of your formal commitments to others and to yourself?
- How do you ensure that you do not overcommit, and instead under-promise and overdeliver, to those around you? How can you direct others to do the same to you?

Chapter 13—Reengineer Your E-mail Practices

- How can you challenge the number of e-mails you send and receive? How can you challenge e-mails that have little substance?
- How can you improve the subject headers you create when sending e-mail, so that readers will understand your call to action quickly?
- How do you make your e-mails more clear and brief so that readers know the requested action and the urgency of your request?
- How do you systematically plow through the e-mails in your inbox so that you minimize multiple touching of the same inputs (e-mails)?
- How do you take control of your inbox so that it is not an indecision box, a procrastination box, a partial To-Do box, or a partial calendar box? How does it once again become a true (unprocessed) inbox?
- How do you "lead change" in others who may have bad e-mail habits?

Chapter 14—Effective Opining

- What is your advice-giving process?
- How do you learn from others so that you will know when they are most ready to receive your advice and your opinions?
- How do you provide permission-based advice?
- How do you ask questions of people so that your advice is not needed? (How do you help THEM find the answers?)
- How do you react to unsolicited advice?

Chapter 15—Are You a Filler-holic?

- Are there common word fillers that you use? How can eliminating them help you become a more polished speaker?
- How can you write in the most efficient and effective manner? How can breaking out the writing process from the research and editing processes improve your written communications?

Chapter 16—Why We Love PowerPoint Slides

- How do you create strong presentations in which the audience is your number one focus?
- How do you clearly articulate your main objective(s) when providing a formal presentation and then reinforce those objectives throughout?
- How do you "mix it up" a little bit when providing presentations to a large audience? How do you grab their attention? How do you make them feel important? How do you let them know that your message and they (the audience) are the show?

Chapter 17—One Way to Avoid Office Rage

- How do you find an outlet for expressing negative emotions that arise from occurrences at work?
- How do you turn anger into problems and then search for solutions?
- How do you confront "offenders" in the most productive manner? How do you focus on actions and solutions?

Chapter 18—Who Is the Puppet Master?

- How much of an impact on your audits can be made when you manage your clients better?

- How do you manage the individuals at your client organization? How do you personalize your service? How do you look out for ways to help them on a professional and personal level?
- How do you make client management planning a standard part of all of your audit planning? How do you prioritize that by spending time as a team creating new client management ideas to implement?

Chapter 19—What Hat Are You Wearing?

- How many different hats (roles) do you wear (serve) when auditing your clients? Which roles are beyond what you should be doing as an auditor?
- How can you capture all those different roles that you serve and the related time involved?
- How can you educate clients best on the actual role of an auditor and show them how you may be going beyond that role?

Chapter 20—Be Memorable

- How do you "write your own stories" of memorable client service?
- How do you enroll clients in defining great client service for you? How do you get them to co-create the criteria used to judge your client service?
- How can you see a client service mishap as an opportunity to build loyalty?
- How can you be yourself a little more in delivering memories to your clients?

Chapter 21—Prepare to Be Fired

- How do you proactively plan "leadership" transitions in your teams (no matter what your level)?
- How do you add new responsibilities to those around you when they are most ready to accept them, and in a position where they want them?
- How do you change your practices in dealing with others so that they know you have a consistently predictable open channel of communication?
- How do you teach your teams to seek problems internally and create team accountability methods for obtaining the results you plan as a team?
- How do you set aside time to reflect on where you want to go and where you want to help others go in their leadership journey?

NOW, WHERE ARE YOU GOING?

The answer to that final question must begin with who you think you already are. BE that person to the fullest. Continue to learn who you are through continued learning of leadership. Continue to be who you are through acts of leadership.

YOU ARE SUCCESSFUL RIGHT NOW, if you choose to be.

YOU ACHIEVE.

Your Plan

- What is the idea I want to implement, or the leadership area I want to improve?
- How does implementing this idea help me to achieve a goal?
- What is that goal?
- How does that goal lead me to become the person I want to be, or uncover the person I already am?
- How will I FEEL once I have accomplished this goal or improved in this area? (Can I anticipate the feelings of success I will have? Can I start to feel them now?)
- How will this be measurable?
- What is the specific next action step I need to take to reach my goal?
- When will I take that next action step?
- What are the other things I will need to do to reach my goal?
- What are the things I will need to stop doing (or give up) to reach my goal?
- What are the resources I need to reach this goal?
- How will I hold myself accountable for doing these things?

Always bear in mind that your own resolution to succeed is more important than any other one thing.

—Abraham Lincoln

You Know You Are an Auditor When . . .

Travel and Vacations

You hold family "planning meetings" before vacations.

You hold planning meetings before vacations, even when it's just you!

You are part of every hotel and airline awards programs in the country.

When playing games with your family or friends, you are always the scorekeeper.

You use vacation checklists so you will not forget anything, and you include items ranging from toothpaste to new auditing guides to your kids.

You buy a book for every new vacation area you are visiting.

Each day on vacation begins with you compiling your To-Do list.

If you are going to an amusement park, you are probably the controller of the park map. If you are married to an auditor, there will be some serious tension related to the use of that map. The map was also highlighted the night before for the most efficient (and effective) paths you will take to the rides the next day. Also, the map is ALWAYS refolded the correct way. Not folding it correctly equals insanity.

You get funny looks from people in other cars as you travel cross-country. (Your bumper sticker reads "I would rather be auditing.")

You feel really bad when you leave feedback on a guest card and you cannot remember the hotel employee's name you are discussing.

Kids

Your kids have adopted the phrase "per discussion with" when talking about your spouse or their siblings. They also use "appears reasonable" when talking about the cleanliness of their room.

You give your kids some nicknames when they do their chores: staff 1, staff 2, etc. Your spouse gets a nickname, also: He or she is the "manager."

Your kids routinely request "extensions" when asked about the status of completing their chores.

Your kids use the phrase "not considered necessary" for the chores they chose not to do. If you have a chore checklist, they efficiently use "NCN." For the chores they do complete, they sign off with their initials, and just as they have learned from you, they "post-date" the sign-off.

You use your label maker to create inventory tags, which you stick on your kids.

You write review comments on their homework.

Their teachers wonder why you always sign your initials and date your kids' book reports.

You demand supporting documentation when your kids attempt to just tell you what their grades are.

Food

You have a folder at the audit site with all the local restaurants' brochures and menus in it.

You have a grocery checklist on your refrigerator with all the foods you buy, sorted by the aisles at your grocery store.

The choice of the restaurant is viewed as the most important "team decision" that needs to be made in any given day.

Your laptop has old remnants of various pieces of food stuck in between the keys. You revel in your ability to multitask by typing with one hand while holding a sandwich in the other.

Career

Your first love was stand-up comedy, but based on feedback, you decided to go in a different direction.

You considered being an actuary but you see yourself as wanting to live a faster-paced, higher-risk life.

You know you are not explaining your audit specialty well when every year your relatives ask you about how difficult "tax season" was and if you can do their taxes for them next year.

You sometimes feel like your career will not be complete until you find a REAL fraud.

Personal Organization

You write tasks on your To-Do list AFTER you complete them, just so you can cross them off.

When you pull out your wallet, you find every single dollar bill neatly folded together and organized in unison from front to back.

When Microsoft Excel expanded from approximately 65,000 rows to 1 million, your life changed.

You stockpile sticky-note pads everywhere in your house, including by the phone and on your nightstand.

You print out your weekly calendar on Sunday nights and distribute copies to your family. They like to note that you are overscheduled already!

You view budgets on audit engagements as "miracle making."

Your stapler has your name on it.

You will actually RE-STAPLE a package of papers if you did not make the "perfect" staple.

You have received numerous messages from IT about the size of your e-mail inbox and how it is affecting network speed (and the speed of the entire Internet).

You keep copies of auditing and accounting guides next to your bed so you can read yourself to sleep.

One creative form of multitasking you do is to complete audits WHILE attending training classes or conferences.

Dating and Romance

Before going out on a first date, you send your date a PBD list.

If you are at a bar and someone approaches whom you would rather not talk to, you pull out your "Hi, I am an auditor" line.

You have tried to convince someone at one time or another that CPA stands for certified professional athlete.

Your spouse typically asks you how your day went when he or she is having trouble sleeping.

Lines NOT to Use When Meeting or Dating Someone for the First Time

My philosophy is: during busy season, showers are optional.

I just finished the worst audit. Can you tell me what day it is?

I am an auditor, trained in the art of understanding how to lie.

Busy season is over for us now. I get to go home again. I hope I remember where that is!

Movies

You exercise professional skepticism while viewing almost all special effects.

You are always telling your family members, "That would not happen in real life!" . . . without even realizing the movie is a cartoon.

Sleep

Sometimes you try counting sheep before you go to sleep, but you always miscount and have to start over again.

During certain times of the year, you do not know what daylight looks like.

You have nightmares about getting your timesheet in on time; you have really bad nightmares about one-sided journal entries, and you have even worse nightmares about lost review notes.

You have dreams about clients who are truly "audit-ready" the first day you get to their office.

You Know You Are an "Experienced" (Old) Auditor When . . .

You know what a "tick-stick" is.

You still have extra green and red lead in your desk.

You remember when a portable computer was taking your desktop from your office to audit site. That was high-tech!

You miss the days where men only wore dark suits and white shirts and women only wore navy blue suits.

You still have your work paper "luggage" carriers.

You can remember numerous fights that broke out over the corner of a piece of paper on which the sign off should be written. You still feel adamant that the bottom right-hand corner is the only real answer.

You can remember several nervous breakdowns you experienced when the debits of a general ledger did not equal the credits.

The word "plug" describes your early career.

You have personally broken more than 10 copy machines at various clients. At least nine times you left the scene.

You have personally killed more than two laptops with "coffee accidents."

The thought of "green bar paper" or an audit work paper that would fold out three times has you reminiscing.

You remember when electronic work papers meant you proactively used Word and Excel (or WordPerfect and Quattro Pro).

When your organization first started adopting electronic work papers, you once lost it and said, "Okay, that's it! I can't take this anymore, we are printing everything out again!"

You still have back problems from carrying work paper boxes.

There are still some old hardcopy work papers in your car, and you are afraid to go back there and see which ones they are because the audits are still unfinished.

You attend happy hours with your younger colleagues, but you fall asleep. You also experience a hangover the next day even though you did not drink.

Your old "10 key" was larger than your current laptop.

You remember when Macs were cool before they were cool again.

When a young staffer asks you if you are "going dark," you get offended.

You are at a level where you do not need to review the general ledger in detail anymore, but you couldn't see it even if you wanted to.

You know what an abacus is because you have used one.

You still have three different kinds of hole-punchers in your closet.

You remember when the "virtual office" was when staff auditors would move boxes and boxes of work papers to wherever the manager wanted to work that day.

You catch yourself beginning many of your sentences with "Back when I was a staff auditor, we didn't have . . ."

You see someone with an iPod in the office and you feel they should be fired.

You still think the Internet is a fad and will go away sometime soon.

You remember the days when you could pick up all the (hardcopy) work papers of an audit and make a judgment on whether enough work had been done based on the weight of the file.

You remember those work papers that documented internal controls that were a copy of last year's work papers with the comment "per discussion with client, no changes." This work paper was recopied for 20 years with just the signatures and the new comment being the only change.

Your folders named JIC or CYA were 20 times thicker than the actual audit files. They are probably still stuffed away in some drawer somewhere, since they were pre-Enron audits.

You fell for the joke as a young auditor when your senior told you to go ask the client if you can count equity now.

You can remember when the per-mile reimbursement rate was less than 20 cents.

Your state CPA certificate number (which is done sequentially) is in the single digits.

You remember when "Casual Friday" was invented.

Afterword and Acknowledgments

The audit profession is fascinating. It produces some of the most ethical, energized, and knowledgeable people on the face of this planet, people who really care about what they do, how they help others, and how they serve clients and the public at large. Sure the industry can be competitive from organization to organization (and in the true spirit of capitalism, that is a good thing!). However, it's rare that I meet someone who feels like the audit industry and those who make up the industry that serve it, are part of a zero-sum game.

Auditors really enjoy sharing best practices with each other, and they go to great lengths to do that. That is clearly apparent at conferences, trade group/association meetings, social networking events/Web sites, and in so many of the auditors I have been able to meet through the years. This book is part of that effort. It is by no means a complete guide to leadership and professional skills for auditors. In fact, it is anything but that. Some of the topics were chosen because they were peculiar and might surprise auditors. Others were just obvious.

If you have not gathered already, this book was not written by an author who considers himself a "super auditor." It is not littered with personal stories about how I did it (and so you should do it this way). Instead, I have been fortunate enough to be a good listener to super auditors who challenge themselves to be better leaders every day. As their leadership coach, I have learned a lot by supporting and challenging them and feel appreciative to share this collection of ideas, practical advice, and tips. The real value of this book, beyond the ideas and tips, comes in the reflection of what you, the reader, are currently doing and the ways you can challenge yourself to take your leadership skills to a new level by uncovering who you are and who you want to be.

When I researched the available books created specifically for auditors, there was very little out there on leadership and other critical professional skills. While some of the areas discussed in this book are applicable for many knowledge workers, it was enjoyable to explore the art of leadership under the microscope of our "little audit world" and examine the unique challenges faced by auditors every day.

Leadership and professional skills like those discussed in this book are typically referred to as soft skills, and sometimes that means people and organizations focus less on them compared with the technical skills we acquire and enhance. What is soft about the skills you uncover and enhance that help you to lead yourself and others to meet your goals (and live your life and realize your dreams)? Beats me. Maybe they should be labeled "critical" skills?

Additional thanks to my wife, Mary Beth, my family, LJC, my coach Keith Rosen, and to Billy Tilotta, Nathan Curtis, Greg Sturgill, Leahmarie Ecle, and Andrew Wright for being a sounding board whenever I asked you to be, and to Ralph Nach for providing that last little push to write this book.

Index